The
Real
America

The Real America

Messages from the Heart and Heartland

GLENN BECK

POCKET BOOKS

NEW YORK   LONDON   TORONTO   SYDNEY   SINGAPORE

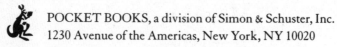 POCKET BOOKS, a division of Simon & Schuster, Inc.
1230 Avenue of the Americas, New York, NY 10020

ISBN: 0-7434-8633-1

First Pocket Books hardcover edition September 2003

10 9 8 7 6 5 4 3 2

POCKET and colophon are registered trademarks of
Simon & Schuster, Inc.

For information regarding special discounts for bulk purchases,
please contact Simon & Schuster Special Sales at 1-800-456-6798
or business@simonandschuster.com

Manufactured in the United States of America

For my Dad, my best friend and trusted teacher

Contents

Contents

The Real America

Introduction

The Fusion of Entertainment and Enlightenment

This truly is the land of opportunity, because if I can write a book, have a major company publish it and people like you actually want to buy it, then anyone can.

It took me a long time to get a radio station to pick up my show, because they didn't understand it. It didn't fit neatly into a little box. I don't talk exclusively about politics. I don't speak exclusively about morality. I don't exclusively screw around. I'm not Howard Stern, Dr. Laura or Rush Limbaugh (first of all, those people earn a lot more money). I tell new listeners that it will take them at least six or eight weeks before they get over their white-hot hatred of the show—and it may take you two hundred pages to get over your hatred of this book. Why?

Because it doesn't belong in the politics, business, comedy, self-help or spirituality sections.

It does belong on your coffee table, nightstand, bookcase or underneath the short leg of the couch. In fact, the capitalist in me wants you to buy enough copies to *build* a couch.

The concept is the same as on the show: I don't think people are one-dimensional. This book should feel like Thanksgiving dinner at your house. You'll talk about politics, life and love. You'll think, laugh and argue. You'll look back with fondness and look ahead with optimism. We all feel a wide range of emotions, and as a borderline schizophrenic, I assure you my range is wider than it should be.

This book is about real life, real people and the real America.

CHAPTER 1

The Real Americans and the Real America

In my faith we have temples, and they are kept spotless and clean. The only place more sacred than the temple is your own home, and your home is to be kept just as clean and in order. Now, I don't mean, "Get out the vacuum, kids!" clean. I mean the kind of clean that keeps something sacred.

In the Real America, the most sacred place on earth is your home, and your home is a refuge. It's a shelter. In the Real America your home is the center of your universe and the center of your home is the dinner table, the most important piece of furniture you have. It doesn't have to be fancy—it just has to be comfortable, so that everybody likes to be in that room and around that table.

In the Real America we will all be very busy—just as we are now—but we'll also be busy doing other people's work, not just our own. We'll be busy helping people—and that doesn't have to mean strangers. That also means we'll help our kids, we'll spend time listening to them, talking to them—just being with them.

In the Real America, we count on the members of our extended family. Our families provide us with an endless supply of hope, love and joy. It doesn't necessarily always happen now, but in the Real America, our greatest support will come from the family and our extended families.

In the Real America, I will be able to change. I will know I can conquer my past and be the person I want to be. We can become better people, and our families will continue to give us support.

In today's America you can do this, but many of us no longer believe it's possible. Ten years ago I was a bitter, hopeless alcoholic who hated people. In a few short years filled with difficulty, but mainly joy, I changed. I am happy now, hopeful, sober, and I only dislike people for really valid reasons. This book is not a self-help book, but by the end of it you will, once again, believe that you can change the world, your business, your family and yourself.

I have found there are four steps to change:

1. You must want it.
2. You must believe it.
3. You must live it.
4. You will become it.

If you read on from here you already want it. Over the coming pages we will focus on the second point. Not only will you believe in the Real America, you will believe that we deserve it and that we can achieve it.

The United States is still a capitalist society, but capitalism in the Real America will be an enlightened way to wealth. Sure, some people will always try to make a buck by squeezing the little people, but in the Real America, I'll be able to make more money—I'll be able to make more of a profit—by treating employees with dignity and giving them access to non-governmental health care and paying them what they deserve. In the Real America, the employee will be a partner and we'll all enrich one another.

In the Real America our current plastic politicians will be replaced by the more genuine, lifelike and human robots in Disney's Hall of Presidents. Actually, partisan politics is a tough topic to tackle, but we will, starting with chapter 4—Everything You Need to Know About Partisan Politics.

Basically, Real Politics in this better America will be based on principle not policy: Real Ethics, Real Values, Real Integrity. As Real Americans, we will not expect to agree with everything a certain politician says, but we will be able to demand that politicians always say what they mean and mean what they say. The Real American Politician will look us in the eyes and say, "Look, Jack, you may completely disagree with me on this one issue, but here are these eight other issues on which we *do* agree. And more important, we agree on principles. And that's just the way it is. If you can vote for me, great. If not, I understand 'cause I don't need this job badly enough to lie to you or myself."

Martin Luther King's dream will come true in the Real

America: a colorblind society—but without political correctness. Unfortunately, King's dream has been perverted and twisted by so many, white and black alike, that it is barely recognizable today. In the Real America, we will know that white men aren't racist; one *man* can be racist. Black men aren't lazy; one *man* can be lazy and racism is not an American problem, it's a *human* problem.

The Real America is the America we all saw on the evening of September 11 and in the days and weeks that followed, but without violence, without sorrow, without mourning. It is an America where the question "How *are* you?" is sincerely asked, and the answer is heard with real concern.

The Real America is a place in our hearts. It's authentic. It's a place we remember. And it's a place we can live in today.

But there are forces keeping us from being the Real Americans and living in the Real America: Now, I'm not one of those people pointing a finger at Hollywood or blaming political correctness or pointing the finger at television or blaming music, because it's not just that.

But it *is* just that. It's *all* of that . . . and one thing more.

The most insidious force keeping us from being the Real Americans is ourselves.

A Different Background Noise

You see, most Real Americans don't even know that they *are* the Real Americans. They've been trapped in a box that other

people built for them, and they think that box is real. They have no idea that it's all a delusion.

It's amazing. David Copperfield couldn't pull this off, and he hooked up with Claudia Schiffer.

So what's the trick? What's the sleight-of-hand?

Somehow, the background noise has changed on us.

Somehow most Americans have been convinced that we don't have the heart we do, that we don't have the power we do. As individuals or a group, this has happened subtly.

When we were kids, we had the *Leave It to Beaver* generation; we had *Gilligan's Island.* I remember watching that show later in life and thinking, "What a stupid show." But I continued to watch it and laugh with it. Mind you—with it, not *at* it. I guess because it was pure.

I mean, there was absolutely nothing really offensive or even challenging about watching *Gilligan's Island,* except perhaps the class warfare between Lovey Howell and Mary Ann, and maybe the hat-slapping abuse on the part of the Skipper perpetrated on Gilligan.

But that was the world we lived in. That was our background noise: soft and silly. Sex was implied in a white, sequined gown, and violence came only in the shape of the Skipper's hat.

Then, when I was growing up in the 1970s, there was a show that almost didn't make it on television: *Three's Company.* Why? Because Jack Tripper lived with two women—and there wasn't even anything going on! But still there were many who thought it was offensive. That's how quiet the background noise was back then. Even *Three's Company* seemed loud.

People will always say, "Look at television today! Look what's happening with television! This is an outrage! This is destroying the fabric of our country!"

No, it's not.

They can put *Three's Company* on, they can put *Friends* on, they can put anything on—name the most offensive television show that comes to mind—how about *The Sopranos*—they could have put that on in our *Leave It to Beaver* world, and it wouldn't have destroyed the fabric of the Cleaver family. Because the Cleavers wouldn't have embraced it. In fact, they wouldn't have even tolerated it, and they certainly wouldn't have invited Tony Soprano into their home at 9:00 P.M. on a Sunday night.

Ward Cleaver is not going to go out to the Bada Bing Club to do blow off a hooker's belly just because he watched one TV show!

But what happened to us between *Leave It to Beaver* and *The Sopranos* is that more of the background noise changed.

In the *Leave It to Beaver* years, the background noises were things like Goodness, Common Decency and Courtesy. You can't even hear those noises any more.

Today the background noise is "Death with Video Games." It's "Rudeness." It's "No Patience." It's "Violent Television." It's "Sexuality Directly Being Marketed to Kids." It's your son laughing as he's shooting a cop in a video game. It's your daughter with a tank top that says *porn star,* hot pants that say *bootylicious* and, of course, underneath . . . the kiddie thong.

Oh, the noise. Listen to it. Look at the billboards. Look at the magazines. See what's on television.

And then look at what you allow in your own home—your temple.

That's why we're having so much trouble. The background noises we allow in our homes keep our homes from being sacred places and keep them from being a shelter from the relentless storm of background noise.

And that's just one part of it. That's where it starts—in the home.

It all starts with Gilligan.

Political Correctness Hasn't Changed Our Hearts

Then comes the classic Great Idea Gone Wrong: political correctness.

Now, as the dad of a child with cerebral palsy, I can tell you that no family is hit more to the core by handicap jokes than the family of a handicapped kid. So when ten or fifteen years ago somebody said, "Hey, let's call them 'handy-*capable*'—it'll make *them* feel better," I thought, "Well, okay, if saying that can make them *feel* better, I don't want to be mean. I don't want to hurt people. I want to live together and be kind and courteous. . . ."

So I got on the bandwagon. "Yeah, you know, handy-capable is not such a bad idea. . . ." I'm into empowering people.

But over time I realized: Handy-capable is as good an idea and as long lasting as Star Jones in a marshmallow boat.

Hey—you're *not* capable, otherwise I wouldn't be building a *ramp* in front of every building in America.

You're not capable of walking up the *stairs*—and that's okay.

So what happens is we start on this good path, with good intent, and we end up head first through the windshield picking the grill of a Mack truck out of our teeth. All political correctness has done is shut us all up. It hasn't changed anybody's mind. Instead it's taken every opinion we have, it's taken every joke that we have, and it's forced us to conceal them and hide them and bury them deeper.

We no longer really *know* what our neighbors think anymore, we don't actually *know* what our co-workers believe— because what they really believe is hidden.

This is a dangerous place in which to dwell. Remember, serial killers are always described by neighbors as "quiet."

Political correctness hasn't changed our hearts—it's just changed our faces.

That's one of the biggest problems we have as Real Americans: What we have in our hearts, we don't share. We've been beaten into feigning bogus compassion by not noticing the difference between me and the guy who should be hanging from a tool belt because he's so handy *and* capable.

We've been convinced that life is all about the superficial stuff. We've been convinced because we see it in commercials, we see it on television, we see it from Hollywood, we see it from our co-workers, we even see it from our own family. It's all about money, power, greed . . . *stuff*. And we think the whole world is like that, because that's the image that we're given all the time.

And so when we're driving in our cars we sometimes think, "I wish I could live in a neighborhood that's quiet and flag-lined, where the neighbors are all next door to one another and they *care* about me and my family. And when somebody moves in, they bake a pie or a cake or a loaf of bread"—like a neighbor did for me—"a neighborhood where, on summer mornings, the air is filled with the sound of screen doors slamming shut as the kids run out to play and mothers' voices cry out, "Just be home for dinner."

But because we no longer speak our minds or hearts, we think that it is just *us* who miss the neighborhoods we grew up in. We never realize we too can bring bread over to the neighbors. We never realize that the neighbors are pining for that too.

I moved into my neighborhood, and this family across the street actually baked a loaf of bread and brought it to *my* family. I didn't know these people from Adam, but they wanted to live in the same kind of neighborhood that I want to live in. In today's cynical world it's tough to know whether to say thank you or test the bread for smallpox.

But the Real America has to start somewhere. Maybe it starts with a loaf of bread.

But when you're driving in your car and you hear someone on the radio saying, "Oh, well, this is what the neighborhood really *can* be like," you *think*, "Yeah, I'd *like* to live like that. . . ."

But you don't say it. You never say it out loud, because you think it's just *you*—that you're being silly, corny or out of touch—because every image you're presented with shows the exact opposite of that.

Political correctness has made us superficial liars. But in the Real America there will be no need for PC because we will talk to one another and those who are handy may just not be capable and vice versa.

Commercialism

Commercialism is another great obstacle standing in our way.

Believe me I know about commercialism. It's my job. If I couldn't get companies to put products on my show that we could sell, I wouldn't be doing my radio show. I'd be selling Hush Puppies and talking into a shoehorn—or I'd be a homeless guy doing card tricks on a cardboard box for booze—or God forbid it would ever get this bad: I'd be a trial lawyer.

And by the way, you just bought this book, so you know all too well that it's about selling people stuff. For us to do that—for me to sell to you—I have to either create a need or else capitalize on one.

For example, you listen to my program because you want this America that I'm talking about. It's a need. You want to believe it's true. And so when I say, "Go out and buy this book," if your need is great enough you will, because this book may help you fill that hole. We do that with all kinds of products from clothes with little Polo ponies to cars with German emblems on the hoods. But your appetite is never satisfied. These things are empty. Perhaps the $25 you spend on this product will break that mold. Because what you'll find between these covers won't make you look cooler or arrive in style, but it may empower you to change.

Well, now, understand that every piece of media you see, everything that spills out of your television, your radio, the movies, your magazines—everything is to get you to buy something. That's the only reason all that stuff exists. That is why in the chapter on business I will tell you that companies in the future can succeed beyond their wildest dreams by breaking that mold—if they understand that we are on to them and that we're looking for real value in our lives. Those businesses that provide quality products with real value and understand the concept of strategic partnerships, will become the Wal-Marts and Microsofts of tomorrow.

But now people are working on you twenty-four hours a day, seven days a week to find your needs, capitalize on them and fill those holes with meaningless junk.

Even more frightening is the realization that our children—now this is new—from the time of birth, are being marketed to. And they're being told they're not cool unless they have these clothes or they listen to this group or they do these things. They're told they're not complete unless they "Obey their thirst," or "Just do it" or "Taste the freshness of. . . ."

And children market to their parents. That's why Disney and fast-food chains market to children, because they know how hard it is for us to say no to our kids.

But going to see the mouse or having the labels read Armani still doesn't fill the gaping hole Madison Avenue has expanded.

And unless we can connect with what is real, our children will get lost. Our nation gets lost because that hunger will need to be fed again and again with materialism, sex, violence or drugs.

I, as a thirty-nine-year-old man, want the new car, whatever it is. Why?

Do you know why the Model T's were all black? Henry Ford wanted to create something everybody would buy *once*. They were all black and you'd buy it once and everybody would have the same thing, until somebody finally said, "Hey, Henry, we can make a lot more money if we start making different models and start souping them up each year. We can actually get people to say, "Well, I have the old one—I'd rather have the new one!"

That's called creating the need. The cars originally were built to last a lifetime. Now they're built with plastic radiators to last four or five years, and it's time for a new one. That need exists, but it is not real.

The reason I hope people will read this book, is that they *know*—something inside of them tells them that this is true, that this better America *exists* and it is not about consumption—it's genuine.

Everything else in the world is telling you it doesn't exist, and the reason it's telling you that is that many of the hucksters have been beaten into cynics or they just want to make money off of you or both.

Cynicism and money have very little to do with the Real America.

TV News

I wrestle with this one a lot, because TV news is very similar to what I do—just with pictures. Even though I am not a journalist—thank God—I am a social commentator. I have to fill three hours every day, and until you try to fill three hours every day on a slow news day, you have no idea what a living nightmare it really is.

It's dental surgery—Marathon Man kind of stuff.

You have to fill the air with something—*anything*.

I have the blessing of being able to fill it—at times—with something of intrinsic value. When there's nothing happening, I can go one of two ways: I can talk about life stuff in a Jerry Seinfeld fashion and do some mindless comedy, or I can talk about life stuff in a philosophical sort of way. So I have the extremes of either pleasant nothing or real substance when TV news is covering just nothing, car chases and partisan politics.

TV news doesn't have my luxury. They have to tell you what's going on even when there's nothing going on. They have to continue to pound that nothing that's going on with "Here's why this nothing is *so important* to you!"

They have to have these overhyped and outrageous TV news commercials where they say things like, "Your children may be *dead* by seven tonight—find out what you could have done to save them tonight at ten!"

It's ridiculous, but to get you to watch, they have to be passionate about everything they cover—and that's impossible. I only have three hours to fill and that's hard enough. But we have three cable news networks going for twenty-four hours a day!

Do the math on that: That's just under seventy-five hours—every day! That's why you see helicopters flying around taping idiots in Los Angeles just driving through their neighborhoods. It's almost to the point where I could expect to see: "Yeah . . . Chopper 7 here with breaking news. We are following a suspect now who has just come out of the Albertsons . . . wait a minute, it looks like the man has some sort of bag. . . . Oh my gosh, Bill, there may be a bomb in that bag. . . . Don't anyone panic, we'll keep watching him."

He went to the *grocery store!* There are *groceries* in the bag. But there's nothing else going on, so they all follow him around in a helicopter!

In our studios, we have ten television monitors to keep an eye on the news channels and it's like clockwork: You'll see one go to the story and then—*bink! bink! bink!*—the other three will go to it too. There will be a small Cessna in trouble and MSNBC will say, TERROR IN THE SKY, and Fox News will say, JEOPARDY IN THE JETSTREAM and CNN will say, REPUBLICANS ABOUT TO KILL SMALL CHILDREN IN CESSNA, and you'll think, "What's happened? Another hijacking?"

What's happened is that a small Cessna over Iowa lost one of its landing gears. WILL THE PEOPLE ALL *DIE*? They'll cover it for forty minutes until it lands and nothing happens. But they will show it and you will watch it because they know you *want* something to happen. You don't want them to die, but they're no longer real people. They have become a TV show.

That's the scary thing about reality television. TV news is the ultimate reality television. You're not watching this because the people in the plane are real people for whom you feel concern—you don't even know who those people are. You're watching it because something *might* happen, those people *might* be killed. The people in the plane become contestants on the real *Survivor,* and we watch to see who will make it and who will not.

Real Americans don't root for people to die.

But TV news is feeding us something, and we're eating it.

So what am I saying? That the people who make TV news are as evil as the people who make Doritos. I want Doritos, but *please stop feeding me Doritos.* I have to beg my children to take away those Doritos or I'll eat the whole bag.

It's the same with TV news. You will sit there, and you will watch it, and you will consume the whole thing, and then nothing will have happened, and you'll say, "Why did they cover that? Why did I watch that? Look at how they hype that up!"

It's just like me eating the Doritos and afterward saying, "I shouldn't be eating those. Why did I eat those? Why did you *let* me eat those?"

TV news is just more empty calories, more background noise, something else that keeps us from being the Real Americans.

Hollywood

Hollywood really needs to have a giant razor-wire fence built around it.

You know, we raised more than $443,000 for the USO for the Rallies for America. My next fund-raising project will be to raise the money to fence Hollywood in, because it's a zoo. They are nothing but weird alien life forms, and some sort of monkey/man hybrids. And like I do at any zoo, I want to be able to visit and gawk at the animals, but we need to make sure none of them escape and roam free in our neighborhoods. They sit in their Malibu beach homes and they have no idea who the Real Americans are.

When Madonna came out with her song "American Life," she actually chastised America and said, "Americans have their priorities in the wrong place. They're all about money, fame, power and sex."

What??? *Madonna* is saying this to me?

I swear, I read that and I thought, somewhere between my bed and the door, there was a wormhole or a parallel-universe gate that I just slipped through, because this America doesn't make any sense when Madonna is pulling a William Bennett on me.

But again, I don't really blame Hollywood, because Hollywood is giving us what we're asking for. We're consuming gleefully what they're serving us.

The problem is: Which is reality? They're giving it to us because we're demanding it, but the Hollywood crowd believes that the world they create for us is the real world.

I'm on the opposite side. I believe that Hollywood shows us our darker side. The real world is the America of goodness, families, values and caring about our neighbors. Not just consuming more sex, violence, fortune and fame.

One of us is right: Either Hollywood knows that this is the Real America, this is the real world, or I'm right. Our core is either the values—the principles, not the policies—of America or it's what you see coming out of Hollywood. It's either "life, liberty and the pursuit of happiness" or it's sex, drugs and rock and roll.

I don't want to live in Hollywood, USA.

Take it all the way down to what some would say is an inane show, the *Gilligan's Island* of our day. Take it down to *Friends*.

Now I love *Friends*. But *Friends* is not real life.

There was a study done that found that average Americans who watch *Friends* actually believe that they have more friends than those who don't watch *Friends*.

They actually consider the people they watch on television to be their friends—subconsciously.

They're not your friends!

They're actors! First clue: It's a fantasy. Who in New York can have the crummy jobs they have and live in apartments like that? And in real life Jennifer Aniston goes for Brad Pitt . . . not Joey and definitely not Ross—because if Ross has a shot, you have a shot. And you *don't* have a shot.

Again it goes back to commercialism: NBC was considering doing an interactive television show where your TV set has a mouse. So, when you're watching *Friends* and you like a lamp, you just click on it. It'll give you the price, put it on your credit card and ship it to you! (Can you click on Jennifer Aniston?)

It's not about entertaining you—it's about selling you stuff.

And it's certainly not about friendship.

That's one kind of lie that comes out of Hollywood, one that we gleefully consume.

The other includes that marriage doesn't matter, that family can be in any shape or form that you want, that the government of America is something that we should significantly distrust and that socialism ain't that bad an idea.

That message comes from the Barbra Streisands and Susan Sarandons of the world—or of HollyWorld. I don't think that lie is as destructive as the other stuff, because nobody really relates to Susan Sarandon or Barbra Streisand. Most people see them for what they are: They're entertainers.

Hey, entertainers: Shut the pie hole and entertain us!

It's the subtle nature of the other stuff, because they present you this picture of this-is-how-life-is and you accept it, assuming that you're just different from everybody else or that there's something wrong with you.

Here's something that I learned early as a broadcaster, something that scared me. For years I did morning radio, and for a time I thought what I did could really be something quite insidious, because I had people in twilight sleep. I had people who would listen just after the alarm would go off.

I was talking directly to their subconscious.

So many times I would hear people say, "You are so funny. I heard you say something this morning but I can't remember what it was."

They were laughing in their sleep. "Ooohhh . . . ," I used to think, "if I would just use my power for good as opposed to evil. . . ."

And that's why when Susan Sarandon comes out and says that she disagrees with conservative values, it's totally fine with me. We are wide awake and her message is clear—just as it is when you listen to Rush Limbaugh. He's not fooling anyone, nor is he trying to. He and Susan are calling it as they see it and are speaking clearly and in no uncertain terms.

The true power hides in the shadows—the subtle lies disguised as pure entertainment or news. Just as I was in morning drive, the writers of *Will and Grace* are talking to people who are mentally half asleep. People are tuning in for entertainment, but they are also getting a message—maybe one they wouldn't necessarily purchase—those messages are only processed through the subconscious. Therefore the viewer begins to tolerate, accept or embrace the moral values of those characters on the program. People love to yell about how dangerous talk radio is. How is that possible? You tune in, knowing exactly what you are getting. Someone with an opinion, spouting that opinion. After that, it's up to you to decide if he is right, wrong or mentally challenged. It's far more dangerous to be presenting a social agenda hidden behind a vehicle that is there just to entertain. The defenses are down, and there is no questioning.

We may be half asleep, but once we recognize the messages around us we can choose what background noise we hear.

Global Scale

Maybe one of the biggest things that stops us from living in the Real America is our global scale.

Fifty or a hundred years ago, your scale was your little home or your farm. I had an old farmhouse that I bought in Cheshire, Connecticut, which was built in the 1800s. I did the worst thing known to man—I bought a house that a real estate agent described as "quaint."

If you're from New England, you know that "quaint" equals "nightmare."

So I bought this "quaint" (nightmarish) little house that needed a "little restoration" (read as: tear it down). Now, growing up in Seattle, where the oldest thing around was from 1920, I had no idea what a 150-year-old house meant, except that it was "picturesque" (read: run down).

It was a home that was built when Millard Fillmore was president. Yeah, *I'm* an idiot.

It all started with a closet: I just wanted a new closet, but once we took that one wall down, the ceiling started to sag, and within twenty-four hours we had to gut the entire house to the outer walls.

It was great. Ever see the movie *The Money Pit?*

But in the wall I found an old letter. When the people who built the house were doing the plastering, evidently they put old things in the walls—newspapers, photos, clothing. I found a letter from a sister of the woman who lived in the house and she said, "I can't tell you how much I miss being at home. I miss the town, I miss seeing you so much, and I talked with

my husband, and we're going to bring the kids out, maybe this Christmas. Oh, how I miss the sound of the sleighbells ringing through the trees and hills."

I thought, "She must be living on the other side of the country. Where could she have moved to?"

The return address on the letter was the next town over, maybe twenty minutes down the road—by car. It's where I would go and get my groceries. It wasn't a long journey for me, but for her, it was the other side of the earth.

That's the way it used to be.

Now the other side of earth *is* the other side of earth—and even that's close. When we can watch somebody in Tiananmen Square stand in front of a tank and defy it—and we're with them, *live*—or when we can see people on the other side of the planet tearing down a statue of a dictator—and our brothers and sisters are there, helping them do it, *live*—that's incredible.

That's no longer the other side of the planet. That's the other side of the street.

But seeing things like war and terrorism live has another effect on us. We see these problems that are on such a huge scale: You've got France and Russia, Germany, the United Nations, Osama bin Laden and George Bush all battling on this global scale while we're sitting there in our homes and easy chairs, eating those Doritos and drinking diet soda. We're watching these global events, and we think we're completely insignificant. We think we can't change anything, because this problem is just too big.

Everything is like that now.

It seems we don't matter anymore.

When the woman who wrote that letter would go in to have her sleigh fixed, she would go to someone who lived right down the street. He knew her and she knew him. They'd talk every day and if the guy didn't fix it right—they lived in the same town, they knew each other—they'd have the problem fixed or they'd have to settle it. Back then, this close sense of neighborhood was born out of necessity.

In the Real America, people will *choose* to care. You've heard of virtual reality. The Real America will exist with a "virtual proximity."

How many times have you sat all day waiting for the cable man to show up? And you know what? They don't have to show up. They don't *care* if they show up. They don't care if you complain. "Stand in line, we'll get somebody else to buy cable and show them our crap." You could burst into flames and they wouldn't put you out if they had a fire extinguisher in their hands.

And that goes from the cable man to the United Nations. It's all the same thing: You're being convinced that you don't matter anymore, that you can't make a difference.

But that's the big lie.

Take it from a recovering alcoholic and drug user, cocaine ain't the big lie. The big lie is that "You don't matter."

You *do* make a difference. Every single person makes a difference.

But you have to want it first and believe it second.

Politics: Policy versus Principle

Politics keep us from being the Real Americans in several ways. (Again, please read chapter 4, Everything You Need to Know About Partisan Politics.) It distracts us from seeing what the real issues are; politics is not the real world—it's just politics.

Now I hear this from people whether they dislike George Bush or Bill Clinton—it doesn't matter who the president is, and it doesn't matter what the party is. The person opposing that person, president or party will always say, "Look at what they've done! You can't trust them! They've done this thing or that thing. They're *horrible!*" And then somebody on the other side will come in and say, "Well, come on, what are you going to do about it? You can't change things—they're *all* like that!"

Well, I'm here to say, "No, they're *not* all like that."

Not all Republicans are clean and dandy, and not all Democrats are scumbags. There are huge scumbags in Congress on both sides of the aisle, and there are good and decent people who really care about America who are Democrats and Republicans.

Partisan politics makes us cynical. It makes us buy into another Big Lie: *that we can't change anything.* The bad politicians need us to believe that. It empowers them.

How many of us would kill for a Lee Iacocca or a Jack Welch to be the president of the United States? Or for the president to approach Jack Welch and say, "Look, here's the six billion pages of the federal budget. Forget about political favors and cut this budget—tell me only what we need and what we don't need. Don't talk politics—just do the right thing for America."

I can guarantee you that we could cut it down. I can guarantee you that the right things would be done and we wouldn't be running a deficit.

I can guarantee you that James Carville wouldn't have a job.

But these things are never done (and James Carville still *has* a job), because there are so few politicians with enough courage to say what they mean and mean what they say.

The Real Americans yearn for somebody . . . anybody . . . to stand up and tell the country, "Damn the consequences from the special interest groups, we're moving forward." Scratch that. There are plenty of people who will *say* that. . . . Real Americans yearn for someone who will actually *do* it. (And they yearn for James Carville not to have a job).

James Carville and Mary Matalin engaged in the most bizarre marriage in the history of humanity. James is the alien talking head of the Democratic party, while Mary spends more time in bed with the GOP then she does with Carville.

It would take a lot for a couple to take the title of "most bizarre relationship" away from these two, but here are a few contenders.

- Woody Allen and Soon-Yi
- Anna Nicole Smith and the Old Dead Guy (He's way too good for her—even now.)

- Camryn Manheim and a salad
- Britney Spears and Glenn Beck
- Celine Dion and her grandfather
- Apples and oranges

Thomas Jefferson and John Adams were having a problem once, and they were arguing about something. I don't know what—maybe Adams said, "Hey TJ, you're a big, fat, red-headed freak," and then Jefferson said, "Oh yeah, well your cousin Sam is a sloppy drunk. And his beer sucks." Anyway, they were arguing about something and they needed to be brought back together again. They needed to come together for the good of the nation.

So Washington came to them and said, "Guys, stop. Listen to yourselves. You're being ridiculous." Boy, would we kill for a Washington now to come to the Republicans and the Democrats and say, "Listen to yourselves!"

But that's what Washington did. He said, "Look, you guys have to come together and *not* think the worst of each other, because, really, you both agree on the essentials. You agree on the principles. You agree on life, liberty and the pursuit of happiness. You agree on the presumption of innocence. You agree that our freedom comes from a divine creator. You just disagree on how much power there should be in the courts, how the Constitution should be interpreted and what the structure of the government should be. That's just *politics*. That's just *policy*. Unite on what brings us together—*principle*."

I'm proud to say that I actually got to see hundreds of thousands of people do just that—come together on principle at my Rallies for America. It was a grassroots effort to show support for our troops that attracted Real Americans in hometowns from coast to coast.

It started with a Dallas morning radio-show host, Darrell Ankarlo, whose son recently signed up for the marines. He asked his dad why there were only protests happening. In honor of his son, Darrell organized a rally to support the troops—3,500 people attended!

I told my callers who were upset that their views weren't being represented in the media about Darrell's rally. I told them to call their local radio station and ask them to organize an event to support the troops. I even promised to show up myself, if they could get it organized.

I wanted people to feel empowered to exercise their right of free speech, regardless of their views on the war itself. I wanted to bring as many people as possible together so our troops would truly know, without a doubt, that they have won the heart of America and that we are capable of setting politics aside and coming together on principle.

Why I Wave the Flag

People say that I am "jingoistic"—which I actually had to look up. I'd like to thank *The New York Times* for calling me that, because *The New York Times* makes me smarter! They call me names I don't understand, and I have to look them up!

So now I've included "jingoistic" on my word calendar. It's my February word. My word calendar has only one word per month, because that's all I can handle. I'm not smart like *The New York Times*.

So when people say that I'm an ultranationalist or that I'm a flag waver, I say, "Yeah, I am." But not because I believe that America is the greatest thing that will ever be or that there is no greater nation on Earth. I just believe that there is no greater *potential* in a nation than there is in America. I believe that we are the greatest nation on Earth *today*—warts, flaws and all. Name a country that doesn't have any warts.

But even that's not why I wave the flag. I wave the flag for the principles of our nation: that all men are created equal, that they are endowed by their creator with certain inalienable rights and that among those rights are life, liberty and the pursuit of happiness. Our principles and our potential: *That's* why I wave the flag.

I wave the flag when I hear the stories of American GIs going into Germany after World War II. Our soldiers rolled into this devastated world with tanks, and they would reach in and hand kids a Hershey's chocolate bar. For these kids, those chocolate bars were their first taste of freedom.

I saw an interview with a woman who remembered that day, and when she spoke, she almost licked her lips, remembering that GI and the taste of chocolate. Now she associates the taste of chocolate with America and freedom.

We went into Japan and when we left, we didn't leave tanks and troops there—we left a constitution. Not *our* Constitution, not *our* system of government—something close to it, but not ours. And you know what? Coupled with the work ethic and the family values of the Japanese, the Japanese kicked our butts economically for a while! And I was one American who wasn't hacked off at the Japanese for doing it—I was hacked off at *us* for not learning more from the Japanese!

When we take life, liberty and the pursuit of happiness and the idea that all men are created equal and give that to somebody else—if that somebody else can take those things and create a better and more effective system of government and enable their citizens to be even more free . . . I vote for that. Show me a better system that enables people to reach more of their potential through liberty and I will show you a system I would vote for.

That's what America is. Not saying, "We are the best, so don't change anything." These concepts, these principles don't come from Americans, they come from God Himself. When you take those principles and build a better system, I'll wave the flag every time.

I remember standing in front of the statue of Abraham Lincoln years ago. Only later did I come to find out that it's not actual size. I looked at him sitting in his chair, and I cried. Now, what did I know of Lincoln? I knew that he freed the slaves, but I was an eighteen-year-old kid from Seattle who grew up disconnected from race riots or white-only water fountains. I didn't cry for Abraham Lincoln or the Civil War, or even the men who died fighting for either side.

I cried for what I can only describe as an unrequited love for an America that is always just out of our reach.

We *know* it's there. It's the passion for perfection, a perfection that we all keep striving for. Americans have never given up. *Never.* We have never said, "This America is good enough," and we never will.

That's the Real America. And I think you're reading this book because you believe that you can help bring it back.

And when I say "bring it back," I'm not sure it ever truly existed. But our reaching for it may have been more focused when we didn't have all the background noise we have now. Nowadays it's more difficult, but we can still reach it if we try.

The Real America is a physical presence that we'll actually achieve if we want it. The Real America is a place where if you're sick, I take care of you—because I *want* to. In the Real America, I will work my brains out, because it's something I *want* to do. I will give freely, not because I'm forced to by the IRS, but I will give my money to others for the good of the whole and my soul.

When every, single member of the community, without exception, chooses for themselves, freely and totally, "that's how I want to live my life," things will dramatically change. That's what the Real America looked like on September 12, 2001: Everyone was looking around for "Who can I help?" "What can I do?" We were *looking* for ways to give away our money—freely, not because we were forced to, but because we wanted to. I stood in line at a blood donation center with hundreds of people in St. Petersburg, Florida—we all had been told there was no pressing need for blood, but we were *looking* for ways to help. And so we gave, freely. We needed the government to protect and defend us. We didn't need some bloated government program to help our neighbors.

That's the Real America. I'm not sure if we can get there tomorrow. But we Americans are extraordinarily powerful individuals. We can accomplish whatever we set our minds to. We can create massive and mighty miracles in our lifetimes. Everything comes from the power of the individual American: Liberty, justice, freedom—our families come from that power; our communities do as well.

Someday we will truly understand that we *are* the Real Americans. And on that day, the whole world will change. And James Carville won't have a job but he'll still have a Republican for a wife.

CHAPTER 2

The Great American Lottery and the Decline of Personal Responsibility

Watch any PG-13 movie, watch it with your kids, and you will know that there is no such thing as a dirty word in America anymore.

I'm sorry—there are two: *personal responsibility.* Those two words have become the "F-words" of our generation.

The decline of personal responsibility started when our greed began to make us all feel as if we were entitled to be the winners of the Great American Lottery. Now this is not the one where you stop by 7-Eleven and buy the little scratch-off tickets.

The Great American Lottery is the one in which you hire an attorney and go to court.

That's the lottery, man! It's the ultimate game show. *Who Wants to Be a Millionaire? You* could be a millionaire!

All you have to come up with is some little problem that *you're not responsible for.*

Real case: Highway 22, Orange, California, late at night. A group of fifteen- and sixteen-year-olds. Mom and Dad are gone, so they decide they're going to raid the liquor cabinet. Then, after a few drinks somebody is lucky enough to find the keys to Mom and Dad's blue Suburban.

So this bunch of freewheeling kids get in the Suburban and drive down Highway 22—but it's raining, and none of them has a seatbelt on. They're drunk—*five years before they're legally allowed to drink in California*—and driving.

They come up around a corner at 55 mph and they hit a puddle, and their car spins out of control. The car flips over and, remember, none of them is wearing a seatbelt. Some of them die; others are badly injured.

What do Mom and Dad do? They call their lawyer.

"Of course it was not *my* child who was at fault. *My child* wasn't killed because he was drunk while underage and driving a car he didn't have permission to drive. He wasn't even killed because he wasn't wearing a seatbelt as the law dictates. No, no, it was not *my* child's fault."

Whose fault *was* it that these sixteen-year-old kids got drunk, took the car without permission, got in an accident, killed some of them and put others in the hospital—whose fault could that have been?

God forbid we actually blame the kids! God forbid the parents take some responsibility!

Here's whose fault their parents said this was: the State of California.

Why? When the State of California was paving those highways, they should have understood that sometimes it rains and that standing water can be dangerous.

Oh, so *that's* whose fault that accident was: the State of California for not properly draining rainwater off the highway.

What a bunch of hogwash.

I'm happy to say the parents did not win this lawsuit, but in the meantime, it cost the state—no, no, I'm sorry, if you're reading this book in the State of California, it cost *you* cash out of your paycheck to fight that.

The reason we all abnegate this personal responsibility in the courtroom is that we *think* we're going to get rich. We *think* there are good odds that Regis will hand us a big check without asking a single question.

Make a pact with yourself right now, and see if you can do it: If something happens to you—whatever it is, but it happens to you and it really is your fault—and an attorney comes up to you and says, "I'm promising you—I can get you ten to twenty-five million dollars if you just follow my advice and go to court," say right now that you'll say, "No thanks."

Are you willing, right now, to swear on this book that if you spill hot coffee on your lap and an attorney tells you he can get you millions of dollars so you'll never have to work again—are you willing to say, "No, I spilled the coffee because I'm a moron"?

That's a hard promise for any of us to make. That's where the greed overtakes our sense of personal responsibility and we start to say, "Hmmm . . . well, really that coffee was a little warmer than it *should* have been." Because who really wants to have an empty wallet and burned genitals? So you start to justify it.

It's the same concept as when we go to the doctor's office for hay fever, and the doctor says, "Let me write you this prescription for Allegra." And you know that Claritin is now over the counter and Claritin has always worked for you. But you say, "Yes, please do. Because if I buy Claritin, I have to pay for it, but if you write me a prescription for Allegra, I can get the insurance company to pay for it."

You think, "Well, I'm only paying five bucks for my co-pay," without really realizing that it's not costing some big insurance company that extra money; it's costing you and everyone else that extra money.

You look at the money you get when an insurance company pays off as "free money." But that's not the way the system works. The more claims, the more expensive insurance becomes.

Not My Kid

If you have a hard time understanding that concept, here's an even steeper hill for you to climb: It's called parental responsibility.

Several stories come to mind recently: a valedictorian in Morristown, New Jersey, a girl with a very high GPA, the highest in the school. But the school district wanted her to have a co-valedictorian, which she thought was unfair, because the other student had a lower GPA.

The school district thought this was reasonable because the first girl, the one with the highest GPA, had a disability that kept her from going to gym classes. Gym class doesn't get the same weighting toward a GPA as other classes do. It gets weighted at a lower level.

Because it's *gym class*.

The first student was allowed to take another elective, and she took a tough class, one that was weighted at the higher level. Thus, she graduated with a higher grade point average, one that no one else in the class was able to reach—because they all had to take gym class!

When the school suggested that she share the valedictorian title did she say, "Okay. I understand. I think that's reasonable and fair"?

Of course not. *She* wants to be an attorney. She wants to go to *Harvard*. She's both handy and capable, it seems.

She went to her folks—and, surprise, her dad is a circuit court judge—and she said, "Dad, I think I should sue. Because this hurts me. I'm humiliated. Really . . . I am . . . well . . . I figure I have endured about two million dollars worth of humiliation." Then she tacked on another million dollars for something else, and she went into battle to be able to be the only valedictorian.

Believe it or not, she won.

Common sense.

Fairness.

Decency.

They don't seem to play roles anymore, do they?

And yet sometimes the universe works everything out. An

update on her story—she was caught plagiarizing, and Harvard rescinded her admission.

The three most obnoxious words in the English language right now are "not my kid."

Hazing. Glenview, Illinois. A group of high school students are chugging beer. They get into some hazing and some of the kids are sent to the hospital. The school suspends these kids for ten days—just ten days!—which means some of them will miss their prom.

Boo-stinking-hoo. They can't attend a prom. Cry me a river . . . as long as it doesn't become standing water that my drunk, underage kids could flip my Suburban in.

Two of the girls actually convince their parents that they should hire an attorney, because they shouldn't have to miss their prom, the school has no right to suspend them for ten days.

My father would have kicked my butt. My father would have first been disappointed, then angry, then humiliated for me—not just *by* me but *for* me.

Is there no sense of shame?

The Death of Shame
Shame 2003

Outdated Feeling

Shame, known by many as that painful feeling arising from the consciousness of something dishonorable or improper, died alone last night of gross neglect.

Shame's many accomplishments over the years are noteworthy. Since the beginning of history, shame brought the United States into World War II, kept people from finishing the ice cream and, until recently, kept hard-core pornography out of the workplace.

Shame has also been responsible for the death of many of history's most disgraceful figures, including Judas, Oedipus and Roman Polanski, who, while not technically dead, currently resides in France.

Shame has been seriously ill for many years, but doctors say it was dealt a significant blow that fateful day in 1995 on the floor of the White House bathroom.

Shame is survived by Conscience, Decency, Civility, Principle and Tact, all of which have been deeply disheartened by Shame's passing. The news of Shame's passing was enough to force the long-suffering friend Honor onto life support.

Funeral services will be held Monday at 7:30 at the McElroy Funeral Home. Graveside services will be presided over by Cardinal Bernard Law. In lieu of flowers, donations can be sent to the National Organization for Women.

You're underage. You're guzzling beer out of a keg, then you're kicking people in a field and covering them with human feces—*and you don't think the school has a right to kick you out for ten days?*

Who the heck do you think you are? You want to talk about self-importance? You are so self-absorbed that you make Donald Trump look like a Franciscan monk.

SPOILED BRAT: "But Daaaaddy, I wasn't reeeeally involved. . . . I was just standing on the sidelines. . . ."

INDULGENT DADDY: "Well, then, you know what we'll do, Honey-pie? Sweetie-Boopie? You know what we'll do after Daddy's little girl wipes her tears? We'll *sue!*"

Well, you know what you *should* do, Honey-Sweetie-Boopie? You should *leave* when you see things like that.

Or you should actually be engaged in stopping people from hurting others.

If you were seen doing *that* on the tape, I *would* hire an attorney and say my daughter was trying to stop it.

"But Honey-Sweetie-Boopie, you seem to be standing there in the crowd, guzzling beer by the kegfull."

Ten days.

Why don't you sit down for ten days? Take your lumps and think about what's really important and what kind of role you play in your own life.

FCATs (Florida's Comprehensive Assessment Test). A kid down in Florida is suing the State of Florida because he can't pass the standardized tests and get into college. He says the State of Florida is hurting his chances of getting into college because he can't get a 40 on a standardized test!

It's not like he's only been allowed to take it once. He hasn't been able to get a 40 in *five tries!*

Let me tell you something, kiddo. If you can't get a 40 on a standardized test in the State of Florida after five tries, you're not going to be able to get a job as a Good Humor Man driving an ice cream truck, with that stupid, little bell all summer long, because you're not going to be able to tell the difference between a Fudgsicle and a Drumstick.

You're a moron. Whose fault is that? It ain't the state's.

It's *your* fault. Apply yourself and pass the test.

Whatever Happened to Common Sense?

The way I know what personal responsibility was like in the old America and the way it ought to be in the Real America comes from knowing my grandfather. I always knew my grandparents were different from me, from a different place, from a different time. They always seemed out of place to me—they even looked at things differently from me.

I remember understanding this when I was about seven years old. My grandfather raised his family during the Depression.

Honestly, how many times would I have to hear about how they used to have *lard* sandwiches every day because they couldn't afford anything else. And Grandma would only spread lard on one side of the bread, to save lard. If I had to hear that Depression story one more time, I was going to close the garage door, start up the car and just start sucking in vapors. Or lard.

But because of that Depression experience, they were different from me, and I first knew that they were different when I was about seven years old. During the summer we used to stay with my grandparents. And on Saturday nights we'd really cut loose. Grandma and Grandpa—wow! That was a wild night! We actually had the opportunity to watch *The Lawrence Welk Show* every Saturday night. We would sit in their old farmhouse living room with their little Zenith television—it must have seemed massive at the time but what could it have been? Nineteen inches at the most?—it was the "console" TV with the little wooden legs.

Grandpa would turn it on and Grandma would have to wait while "the set" warmed up. Finally, the picture would come on, and we'd get to watch *The Lawrence Welk Show* with the accordion, bubbles and Larry himself dancing with the old ladies.

That was great fun, my grandparents thought, for us.

Grandpa walked in one Saturday night, and he stood in the doorway in between the kitchen and the living room, and he said to us, "Kids, who wants ice cream?"

And my sisters, who were the smart ones in the bunch—they knew my grandparents better than I did—they said, "Sure, Grandpa!"

I was the one who was never really quick on the draw. I said, "What kind?"

And I'll never forget seeing my grandfather stand there in the doorway and look at me like I was an alien life form. He looked at me like I was from another planet, trying to figure out what the heck did that question even *mean.*

"What *kind* of ice cream?" he asked, not trying to be mean.

Then he looked at me, still puzzled, and gave me his only answer: "The kind you eat."

He was just different from me.

He was the kind of guy who, were we to drive through McDonald's, and were I to order hot coffee and then spill the hot coffee on my lap because I was moron enough to hold the hot coffee between my legs, the last thing in the world he would ever think to say would be, "You know what, Glenn? I think we should hire an attorney."

And if I wanted more coffee, he would have been my own personal warning label. He would have then proceeded to make fun of me every time we drove through a McDonald's. He would have said—lovingly but firmly, "Don't forget, dumb-dumb-dummy, it's *hot* coffee you just ordered."

I don't believe that our parents and grandparents needed to have a label—and I've actually seen this label: SNOWBLOWER SHOULD NOT BE USED ON THE ROOF.

No, really? Snowblowers *shouldn't* be used on the roof?

I don't know if it's a gene that they just didn't pass on to us. I just can't figure out why it no longer occurs to us naturally that snowblowers should not be used on the roof or that hairdryers shouldn't be used in showers, but our parents and grandparents got that instinctively.

And if they would have used a hairdryer in the shower, again Grandpa wouldn't have called up Norelco and said, "Why the heck didn't you put a label on that? My wife didn't understand she couldn't blow-dry her hair and put the suds in at the same time."

He would have just said, "What are you, a freaking

moron? Stop, wash your hair, get out of the shower, dry it with a towel and then use the blow dryer."

So I think personal responsibility the way our parents and grandparents understood it was really just common sense.

Whatever happened to common sense?

R.I.P. Common Sense
Common Sense 2003

Common Sense, the type of information many people believed you were born with, was pronounced dead last night on the floor of the United Nations Security Council. Several high-ranking government officials were there, but nobody noticed its passing for several hours.

For years, Common Sense was responsible for many Americans not using a toaster oven as a bath toy, taking off their clothes before ironing them and not jumping off their roof with a broomstick between their legs after reading Harry Potter.

In the early 1970s, Common Sense began noticing symptoms of his fatal illness when Evel Knievel kept mounting his motorcycle after having broken every bone in his body at least once. Symptoms worsened in the mid 1990s during a lawsuit by a woman who was burned by coffee. The final blow came in 2002 with the premiere of NBC's hit reality show *Fear Factor*.

Common Sense is survived by Litigation, its dysfunctional step-cousin. In lieu of flowers, Litigation asks that you send broken glass to children.

Whatever Happened to Summer?

In the world of our parents and grandparents, each person was responsible for himself or herself.

But we were also responsible for one another—without attorneys.

The giant corporations were not responsible for my safety. I was responsible for my safety, and my parents were responsible for my safety.

But personal responsibility gave way to "personal liability" and we lost many aspects of the world of our parents, many freedoms and abilities that enriched their lives. We lost the ability to do things they used to take for granted.

Like somehow, we lost summer.

I remember summers.

I can remember the sound of the screen door as it slapped back against the front door as I was running out of it. And after that sound in my memory, there is always another sound, the sound of my mother's voice calling out, "Just be back in time for dinner."

That could have been said to me as a ten-year-old kid at five o'clock in the afternoon or seven o'clock in the morning. During those carefree summers, we could run outside and play and get lost and my parents' only concern was "Be back in time for dinner."

Can you even imagine today, living in *any* city, and saying to your ten-year-old kids at nine o'clock on a summer morning, "Be back in time for dinner. It's going to be around six"? Never.

The reason our parents could say that is that we *knew* each other. We knew the neighborhoods, and we knew the neighbors. And, more important, the neighbors knew *us*.

And so we would run down the street and we knew which yards to be careful of, because, for instance, down at the end of the block was an old, gray house with an old, gray lady named Mrs. Olsen, and if I were doing anything wrong, she would be the first one on the block to open up her door—and I remember the sound of *her* screen door opening and closing as well—and she would call out, "Glenn Beck, you stop that right now! I know your mother wouldn't want you doing that!"

And I would stop, because I knew that Mrs. Olsen was going to be on the phone with my mother. I never remember Mrs. Olsen ever coming over to our house. I never remember going over to her house either. I don't even know how my parents knew her, except that she lived on our block. It's funny. I don't ever recall seeing her outside of that door frame with the screen door pushed open.

Mrs. Olsen wasn't mean. In fact I believe just the opposite. She was just the lady down the block, keeping an eye out for us kids and certainly not because Mrs. Olsen was afraid that we would fall off her tree and *sue* her.

So what happened?

Somehow our greatest asset as Real Americans, our greatest strength, our greatest attribute—that we are always looking forward, always looking ahead—got in the way. We wanted to make things better for *everyone*.

And so we started thinking about how we could help others and somehow we got involved with something that came to be known as "political correctness." Who wants to be mean to the poor, little, handicapped kid in a wheelchair? Nobody does. So, we decided to help him out.

Then the government decided to help him out too. That's when it turned into a nightmare.

Smoking is a good example: Let's get the government to stop this evil corporation from packaging tobacco products and saying that it's good and it's fine when indeed they knew all along that it wasn't good and fine.

Now everyone agrees that the company should be reprimanded. So the government tells them they have to tell us: "These are killing you, but if you want to smoke them, God bless you. We're here to make money, so we'll sell them to you. Smoke all you want but just know so that we all clearly understand: *They're killing you.*"

Okay. We wanted to make sure that the companies were held responsible and that was taken care of.

But what happened then is that it got to a point so far beyond reason that *individuals* were no longer required to engage their brains.

Now the companies would be responsible for the guy who wanted to get up on the roof with a snowblower.

I'm sorry, nobody can protect you from being an idiot. If

you're an idiot, you'll always be an idiot, and if anybody's responsible for it, it's your mom and dad, not a company. Your mom and dad apparently didn't raise you well enough to know that when you want to remove the snow from the roof, it's best to climb up there with a shovel.

The Question of Oreos

So how did we go from sharing responsibility to worrying about liability?

The greatest veil on seeing the truth is time.

Things always go from good to bad gradually, and the change usually starts with a good reason. You can never pin when a good thing turns bad. It's usually not until it's full-fledged bad that you say, "Gee, we have a problem here." So I don't think this was something that changed overnight. It is the background noise that is changing us.

For instance, when did you start drinking bottled water? Can you remember? I remember the first time I walked into a store and said, "Bottled water for a buck? What are you, nuts? Who the heck is going to buy a bottle of water for a dollar?"

Yet I can't remember when, but I started drinking it myself—and now it's completely acceptable. But I remember when I thought it was an insane idea.

It's the same thing with trying to pin down the end of personal responsibility. Why didn't we see it coming? When did we realize we lost it?

Again, our grandparents wouldn't have needed a label on a

box filled with Styrofoam packing peanuts that says—and again, I've seen this—DON'T EAT THE STYROFOAM.

When did that happen? At the same time we all started drinking bottled water for a buck a bottle, I'll bet.

You know the story about an attorney who wanted to stop our children from having Oreos—he actually wanted to take the Oreos off the shelves—because there are too many "trans fats" in them.

Now I'm not even sure what trans fats are, but I'm pretty sure that if it's bad, it's in an Oreo cookie. I think I knew that the first time I had an Oreo cookie, because I understand the concept of God: God makes all things I like bad for me. Chocolate. Sugar. Butter. Cream. Mmmmm . . . creamy chocolate sugar butter. If it's bad for me, I will love it, and I love Oreo cookies.

They say that the trans fat makes the cookie part crisp and the creamy stuff creamy. If that's true, I want *everything* covered in trans fat. And you know what? If I choose to feed my child Oreo cookies washed down with a big old glass of bacon fat—hey! that's my business. I have to be a big, fat moron to think that I'm doing my kids a real service by feeding them a bag of cookies, and a glass of bacon fat and thinking that's healthy.

In moderation, everything's okay. (Okay, not Drano, rat poison or pâté.) If I'm the parent who thinks that Oreo cookies are healthy, then I must be the same parent who thinks that Cap'n Crunch is really good for my kids too. Because, after all, he's a cap'n! He wears a uniform and a man in uniform wouldn't lie. . . . Would he?

I laugh when I walk into a McDonald's and see a McSalad. What a McJoke.

Who goes into McDonald's for something healthy? I don't go to McDonald's because that evil clown, Ronald McDonald, hypnotized me when I was little. I have known, for a while now, that McDonald's wasn't the most healthy food for me.

I look at my big fat face in the mirror and I know I shouldn't be going to McDonald's, Taco Bell or Burger King for lunch every day—unless I want to continue to be fat.

I'm pretty clear that students at UC Berkeley believe that Ronald McDonald is, in some way, out to kill me—because he's a capitalist. But unlike most capitalist murderers, I welcome Ronald McDonald with open arms.

Like *The Matrix*. There's the blue pill and the red pill. Which one are you going to take? My brain gives me an option. Am I going to have the McDonald's or am I going to have the granola and sprout salad at the local Curd Counter? Which am I going to do?

I will choose the Quintuple Quarter-Pounder with Bacon and Ranch, and a side of blue cheese with my French fries every time—and *I'm the only one responsible for that decision.*

And I know that to be true, every time I look down and see my middle torso covered in twelve inches of McFlab.

I'm the one responsible. I could eat cauliflower—or I could eat *flour* . . . mixed with a few eggs, some chocolate, some sugar, a creamy filling . . . ooohhh, some icing and some sprinkles . . . *mmm,* creamy chocolate sugar butter—my favorite!

I'm aware of both options: cauliflower or flour.

I choose the flour, and I happily accept the responsibility of shaping both my life and my big fat butt.

I am also aware of those pale-skinned, anorexic sprout-and-bean-curd-eating vegans who want me to stop consuming anything that has a face, yet they will run to any attorney who will help them suck the very life blood out of the happy little clown known as Ronald or the royal king of the burgers.

The Big Lie

It was not the Colombian drug lord who made me snort cocaine. It was me.

It was not Jack Daniel's who made me take a drink. It was me.

It was not the guy pouring the Bacardi who put me behind the wheel. It was me.

What's totally insane is the idea that some pimply faced kid who's working at Chili's and making $2.12 an hour and asking you questions like, "Would you like to try our new Awesome Blossom?"—what's insane is that this kid is "responsible" for making sure that I stop pounding back margaritas and saying to me, "Hey, Fatso, why don't you put down that Awesome Blossom and count how many fricking empty glasses there are in front of you. Don't you think you've had a little too much?"

Why should *he* be responsible if I drink and drive? *I'm* the one who's ordering the drinks!

It's as nuts as Dennis Miller saying "these two teams are more like 'worlds in collision' than Immanuel Velikovsky could ever have imagined" and *expecting* the average football fan to get it. Having a prepubescent waiter be responsible for keeping me skinny and sober is not only nuts, but it also goes against everything that America really stands for: the rights of the individual.

Okay, so let me admit early in the book: I have a problem.

In fact, I have the same problem as President Bush.

It seems that President Bush, a man whom I deeply admire and respect, delved into some of the great things that I did— *allegedly.*

But there is no alleging *my* use of illicit drugs and alcohol. If I hadn't been such a cheapskate, cocaine would have killed me.

I remember looking into the mirror one day and seeing crusted blood all over my face, from all the cocaine I had snorted the day before.

Man, that's one drug you never forget to take your dose of. I mean, you take one dose and ten or fifteen minutes later, you're thinking, "Hey, when's the next?" If cocaine were prescribed, they'd have to use the opposite of the instructions they usually use on prescription medicine: On antibiotics, the instructions are: TAKE EVERY 12 HOURS. On cocaine, it would have to be: DO NOT TAKE BEFORE 15 MINUTES. And you'd never have to use the sticker that said: FINISH ALL MEDICINE.

So I remember standing in front of that mirror and thinking, "I just spent two hundred dollars to feel like this. I don't *ever* want to have anything to do with that again." So I found other recreational drugs, like alcohol, to get into that were much more cost-effective and didn't make my nose bleed. But it went on for a very long time.

Now I find myself in the position that George Bush is in (except I'm not the most powerful man in the world): I have to tell my children not to do what I admit I did.

I have to look at my kids and say, "How do you *not* make the same mistakes I did? How do I tell you how to do that?"

My religious beliefs help me do that. So does my history: I'm an alcoholic and my mother was an alcoholic who committed suicide.

I can tell them that there was a bridge abutment in Louisville, Kentucky, that had my name on it. Every day I prayed for the strength to be able to drive my car at 70 mph into that bridge abutment. I'm only alive today because (a) I'm too cowardly to kill myself—that actually takes more courage than I had—and (b) I'm too stupid. I only thought about violent suicides like the bridge abutment thing and putting a gun in my mouth while listening to Nirvana. I never thought about quiet suicides like overdosing on sleeping pills or eating too many Oreo cookies.

I would probably be dead or at least really fat by now if I had thought about doing it that way.

So I have those stories to tell my kids and say, "Look, insanity runs in the family like a pack of wild elephants. Don't turn out like Grandma. Don't turn out like me."

But if George Bush looks at his two daughters and says, "Don't turn out like me," they'll probably say, "Dad, you did cocaine and alcohol, and now you're the most powerful man in the world. I'm only doing pot and drinking—geez, at this rate I could be queen of the universe by Tuesday."

It's like everything else, they'll have to find answers their own way. Ultimately it is *their* choice and they will have to become responsible. As much as I wanted to think, when I was drinking, that my problems came from cocaine and other things and other places and other people, that was just a big lie.

Cocaine is not the big lie. The big lie is blaming our life's messes on others. I may have had bad things happen to me, but I am more than just the sum of the roadblocks I or others have placed before me. Because no matter what others tell me, I am in charge of my life—not them.

My problems began and ended with me. I needed to take responsibility for what I had done, what I had thought and what actions I took. Once I took responsibility for those things, I could then start to deal with them and sort them out. I could put them in their proper place and perspective.

Instead, we have people who want to blame other people and other things. But let me tell you something: If Jack Daniel's were responsible for my drinking, I'd own Old No. 7 by now. I would probably own half of Tennessee. Jack Daniel's is not responsible—*in any way*—for what happened to me.

But there are people now who blame everything on everybody else, and more important, they end up expecting so little from themselves—and so little from their children—that they go out and say, "You know what? My kids are going to drink anyway, so I'm going to get the booze for them. As long as they're doing it in my house, I can control them."

In my house, I expect my kids *not* to drink. That doesn't mean my kids are going to be perfect. That means I *expect* my kids *not* to engage in those activities, with the hope that it becomes a self-fulfilling prophecy. If you expect your kids to drink and have sex, I guarantee a self-fulfilling prophecy. I take responsibility for my own habits and my own household. If I'm going to tell my kids that alcohol is dangerous and they have to be responsible with it, then I better be responsible with it myself, because their biggest teacher is me.

Ultimately, that will teach them two lessons: one about alcohol and the other about personal responsibility.

Why Libertarians Are Only Half Right

The libertarians actually have it right. Unfortunately, they're about a billion years too early in the evolution of man.

In a utopian society, there should be almost no government. The government should provide for the common defense, build roads—that's it. We should be doing everything ourselves. Why? Because we choose to.

I should have the option of going into a store and buying cocaine.

But I wouldn't go into the Macy's Cocaine Department and get some Ralph Lauren Nose Candy, because it wouldn't be the responsible thing to do. Sure, it looks great with the little

Polo pony on the spoon, but it's not good for me mentally, physically or spiritually. So I wouldn't buy it, because it's not good for me or for our society: It's also not good for our children. It's not good for a myriad of reasons.

But we're not at that point, and the further we go down that PC road, the further we go down the lack-of-personal-responsibility road, the more we happily pad after a Perry Mason—nightmare-attorney culture, the further we get from the utopia where you don't need big government.

Keep suing and saying, "Not my kids," and watch how enslaved you become, because big government will always treat you like a five-year-old kid. I don't know about you, but I'd like a little more freedom than I would give to my five-year-old. I'd like to be able to say, "Yes I know, I probably shouldn't stick that knife into the toaster to release the bread, although I have a right to." Common sense tells me that I should *choose* not to.

The only reason we're going down that road is not because we think it's the right thing to do, but because most Americans now see the American justice system as "The litto Lotto." The courts have become nothing more than a litigation lottery system. I can go in, put my buck down and come out a bazillionaire. How great is that? I've been trying that with my dollar at the gas station lottery and it doesn't work.

But I can just put my snowblower on the roof if they haven't told me not to, fall off, and become a bazillionaire. Hmm . . . I might be willing to go blow the snow off my roof to get that.

That's what this is all about: money, because we prize

money more than anything else it seems. Remember: It's the economy, stupid.

Real Americans don't make money their goal. Money is neither good nor evil. It just is. And it is an easy vehicle to create or destroy.

When it comes to litigation and personal responsibility, the temptation of winning big money in the Great American Lottery is destroying us, not building us up.

Taking Responsibility

My mom and dad were not responsible for everything bad that's happened in my life.

My mom was a drug addict who committed suicide when I was thirteen. While that was a horrible and tragic event in my life, one that took me years to get beyond, in many ways it has ended up helping me become the person I am today. I am stronger because of it. I am wiser because of it.

So many people think that you spend your whole adult life just trying to recover from your childhood. You can either choose to look at it that way, or you can take responsibility for where you are right now: What did I learn from that experience? Although it may not seem positive now, what is it that I can bring from that experience to make my life more positive right now? That's where responsibility kicks in.

All parents want to make the road easier for their kids. They want them to have a better life than they did. They want their kids to be protected. That's normal.

I went to the Vanderbilt mansion in Newport, Rhode Island, a few years ago and I saw one of those little brown national historic signs that are everywhere. The inscription said that Vanderbilt had a problem with how to educate his kids.

He felt that everything that made him a great man was not part of his children's lives. Because what made him a great man was the struggle. Now that he had succeeded, his children didn't have to struggle. "Hey, Dad, are we going to have the freightload of silverware put on the private yacht or the private train when we go to Newport?" That was their big struggle—they didn't have anything to struggle against. So in giving them everything, Vanderbilt realized, he'd actually given them nothing.

Political correctness and the decline in personal responsibility have worked together to harm our kids. By taking these things away from our kids, by telling them that they're never going to get hurt, that they don't have to take responsibility, that they're never going to get into a situation in which they might be offended, we've actually made them weaker.

It's like what we do with antibacterial soap: Doctors now say that your body should be able to kill on its own any germ you're killing with antibacterial soap. So all you're doing is making those germs stronger and the body weaker.

View "blame" as a bacteria and political correctness as the soap for a minute. In the past, if somebody called a handicapped kid "Hey, Gimp!" the kid's mom would say, "Oh, I'm sorry, baby. That happens. But remember: 'Sticks and stones may break your bones but names will never hurt you.'" And that kid would be stronger the next time. But with the anti-bacterial soap of PC cleansing out the easy struggles, the body becomes less capable of dealing with the everyday struggles and a sitting duck for a killer bug.

Now, we want to sue that taunting kid and get even, which is a natural reaction on the part of a *parent:* to protect your children. But when the government does it, it's infantilizing. And if your kid can't handle "Hey, Gimp, why don't you run and tell Mommy?" how is your kid going to be able to handle the real world?

Personal Responsibility and Abortion

I used to be a social liberal and fiscal conservative, like Thurston Howell: "Uhhh, Lovey and I are *fiscally* conservative, but socially, well, *anything goes!* Right, Lovey?"

I was absolutely pro-choice: I believed a woman had an absolute right to choose. I believed it was her body and her choice, and I think I had that point of view mainly because I didn't want to take that option off the table for myself. The reason I was pro-choice is that I don't know if I could really have said in a situation like that, "No, don't kill the baby." It never came up, but I don't know what I would have said if it had. I also lean libertarian at times—we should have the choice but never use it.

But then when I started to get my life in order, the first thing that I took a look at was my own sense of personal responsibility. As a recovering alcoholic, one of the first things you do is say, "Okay, I'm completely out of control and I need to find a higher power to help me through it. Then I need to start making inventories of all the crap I've been doing."

As I started working on my own sense of personal responsibility, trying to find consistency in my new understanding of responsibility, I began to look at a wide array of issues. Abortion was one of them.

To me the debate about abortion became that you made a choice. You and the guy you had sex with made a choice to have sex. One of the many things that can happen when you have sex is that you could—call me crazy, but I think this *can* happen—get pregnant.

If you get pregnant, well, your choice has *already* been made. Parents who would support their pregnant children getting an abortion, which is actually crippling them, are taking the repercussions of their kids' actions away. They are removing any sense of personal responsibility from them.

When I was a high school senior, I had to take a class called "Rights and Responsibilities." Do they even have that class in high school anymore? Or is it just called "Rights" now? That class taught us that our rights are coupled with our responsibilities, and if you don't engage in the responsibility part, *your rights will go away.*

That's the whole balance of the deal.

That's where the libertarians have it right. If everybody's responsible, we all have unlimited rights. But if you're not responsible, if you're a forty-year-old baby, then you've got to be treated like a baby.

When you've engaged in sex, it's time to pay the piper. That doesn't mean you raise the kid, but it does mean you have to *carry* the kid.

Full term. See you later.

I'm against abortion for a myriad of reasons: The first is that I want my child to be stronger from the mistakes he or she makes. You've got to learn from your mistakes, and the only way you learn from your mistakes is if there's a consequence, if you somehow or another go through some fire.

When people meet me, they usually say something like, "You're so young—I thought you were *much* older." And I appreciate that, really I do—what, do I sound like Larry King? The only reason I think people say that—other than the fact that's there's not a hip bone in my body, except the ones that are attached to my legs—is that I've had many experiences that have led to my developing a fine sense of cheesy wisdom.

My wisdom doesn't come from being a smart guy. It doesn't come because, *ommmmm,* I sat on a mountaintop with Richard Gere and we talked about life, man and the universe. My wisdom comes from falling on my face over and over and over again. I make Chevy Chase look graceful when it comes to experiences in life. I continually fall on my face, but it is that very falling on my face and the act of picking myself up and shaking my head and saying to myself, "Holy cow! What an *idiot* you were for doing that"—that helps me make sure I won't be so stupid next time.

That's the only thing that gives me wisdom, and just like Vanderbilt, I cannot pass that experience on to my children. I can help steer them, I can help move them in certain directions, I can protect them from certain things. But in the grander scope, I can help my children best by teaching them to take responsibility for their actions, both good and bad.

As a society, our greatest strength is to look forward and to say our better days are ahead of us and—you know what?—I struggled hard and I want to make sure my kids don't have to. But by doing so, you disturb a very delicate balance and if you don't do that in the right balance, you destroy the future of your children.

That's where we are now, but hopefully, we're waking up to it.

We've got to come full circle with that bottled water. We first looked at the bottle and thought, "Who would pay a dollar for that?" But at some point in America, we will come to a point where we will once again say, "A buck for water? And I could just go to the tap?" And we will come back full circle.

But something painful needs to happen, something needs to cause us to come back.

I believe that's already happening. I believe our society is already starting to see the beginnings of the end of the decline in personal responsibility. And we have to continue that, or we destroy a very bright future.

Abortion is the toughest question to answer when it comes to your own family. I like to think I'd have the courage of my convictions to help my daughter do what I believe is the right thing, but I can't be sure. Just as I can't be sure how resolute and brave I would be if I were called upon to serve my country in the military. I've always been afraid that I would be that guy in *Saving Private Ryan* who's on the stairs, paralyzed and crying as his friends are being killed.

I don't know how to predict what I would do, but I know that abortion would not be the answer. I don't know exactly what I would say to my child because I would be filled with so many emotions: disappointment in her but, even more so, disappointment in myself. What have I done wrong? How have I not been there for my kid? How did I not see the warning signs?

So I don't know how I would react—*initially*. I know that once I got control of myself, I would absolutely say, "You have to bear the child."

Hypothetically, though, if my daughter came to me, what I would hope I would do is, first, sit down with her and give her a hug and tell her that I love her and that we all make bad decisions.

I would remind her that I am a man who's made a pack of bad decisions in his life.

"But," I would tell her, "you made a decision. You're an intelligent girl. You knew exactly what was going on, and you knew what the odds were. Now you know spiritually what the right thing to do is, because I raised you to know that. And you know what I believe about personal responsibility— you've been raised to take responsibility for your own actions. This is not somebody else's fault.

"So I highly recommend that you have the child and put it up for adoption.

"If you're adult enough to conceive this child, you're adult enough to make these decisions. After all, you do have a choice: You could raise the child.

"Know that if you keep this child, it could destroy any real future that you have. More important, it could destroy the child's future of being raised in a stable home with financially secure parents, who are adults.

"So give the child away. But carry your baby to term."

And if she were to say that having the child was not her choice due to rape or incest, I can't fathom saying, "You have to carry it anyway," personally because it would make me a monster to continually traumatize my daughter as she would be raped every single day that child was growing inside her. But there is something in me that I can't quite quell that says, "It's still life."

I am clearly for abortion in the case of incest, rape and saving the life of the mother. I am clearly standing there in support of those rights.

But there is some echo inside of me that keeps bouncing around in my soul that says, "That's not quite right."

I don't know how to rectify those things.

I guess no matter how hard I try to be consistent, I am still just a dad.

And I take responsibility for that.

CHAPTER 3

Celebrities in America

My problems with celebrities in America are not just with the individual celebrities, although, oh man, I could probably do four hours nonstop—no commercial breaks—on Barbra Streisand alone.

Now to understand my true feelings for Barbra Streisand, you first have to understand that I hate cats. Not only the Broadway show *Cats,* but also the animals themselves. That said, I would rather live in a world inhabited entirely by nothing but cats, just them and me—with the entire feline population standing on my kitchen counter forcing me to endlessly listen to their four-legged version of Michael Crawford screeching out "Memory"—rather than listen to five minutes of anything that spills out of Barbra Streisand's mouth.

Sometimes I just feel like screaming, "Shut up, you big-nosed, cross-eyed freak!"

Then I remember that wouldn't be very Christlike of me. Nowhere in the Bible does Jesus call anyone a "big-nosed, cross-eyed freak." However, one must keep in mind, Jesus didn't have to live in a world with Barbra Streisand . . . or Hollywood.

My problem is not only with the individual celebrities like Striesand—and don't worry, Michael Moore, you're going to get your shot later on in the chapter—it's with the whole celebrity culture. These people are so out of touch or have been so hypnotized by the "glamour" of Hollywood—and if you've ever been to Hollywood Boulevard, you'll know how glamorous nipple rings, homelessness and dirty needles can be—that they actually start to buy their own scripted lines. They buy their own garbage.

Let me just set the stage on what little I know about buying your own garbage. When I was doing the Rally for America to support our troops in Iraq, I was going from city to city, arriving in a plane, sometimes a private plane. A limo would pick me up at the airport, whisk me to the venue, where I would be greeted by throngs of people who just wanted to shake my hand and say, "Do you know how much I agree with you?" and *"Blah blah blah, blah-blah blah-blah."*

Then I'd go onstage and I would talk for about thirty minutes to about twenty-five thousand people. And I would say, *"Blah blah blah, blah-blah blah-blah,"* and they would say, *"Cheer-cheer-cheer."* Then I'd get offstage, and again I'd be mobbed by the crowd, who just wanted to say, "You are so great" and *"Yada-yada-yada"* and I'd get whisked to the airport and get back on that plane and think, "Wow! That town *loves* me!"

The Real America

What a heaping pile of crap that is.

> Knock, knock.
> Who's there?
> Orange.

These people who are coming out are a microcosm of that city. They are coming out because they are the ones who agree with me. That doesn't mean they love me—it means those twenty-five thousand people responded to a message. And maybe five thousand of the twenty-five thousand actually have a clue as to who I am and really are fans. But still, those five thousand were there for the troops and the message, not for me. I didn't always understand this. In my early twenties I was a highly successful morning-show host, and I really started to buy my own hype. By the time I was thirty, the crowds were thinner than my hair and I bottomed out. It was really at this time that I began to understand "celebrity."

Sheryl Crow walks onstage in front of twenty thousand people, and she thinks, "Oh, these people love me. These people *want* to hear my message."

No, Sheryl. They want you to come out with your shirt half open, and they want to hear you sing "All I Want to Do Is Have Some Fun."

Nobody *cares* about your opinion, Sheryl. You are paid to sing songs about the Sun coming up over Santa Monica Boulevard. That being said, please understand the opinion of a citizen of Hollywood is worth no less or more than yours or mine. I know that, and you know that. But I'm pretty sure that Natalie Maines is still missing the epiphany on this point.

What kills me is that celebrities don't "get" this, and yet I understand that when all is said and done nobody really cares about my opinion either—and I'm *paid* for my opinion.

It's the illusion the Amazing Keller couldn't have dreamed: that *you* actually care what *they* think because of what *they perform*. And here is how this becomes an endless loop: Because of what they do, because of their celebrity and money, they must endure necessary, self-imposed isolation. Not isolation from everything, mind you, just isolation from the Real America and people like you. They have to live with guards, gates, guns—unless they're Rosie O'Donnell.

Oh, no, I forgot: Rosie may be against everybody else having guns but she gets some for her own protection.

Honestly, in some ways I feel sorry for celebrities, even though they have great riches. The little things that we take for granted, they can't do. They can't just go out on Saturday night to a movie theater and get pissed off like we do because the high school kids are talking all the way through the movie. They don't get to enjoy those little subtle experiences that we get to enjoy. They have to be protected from society.

Well, when they're really protected from society and wildly cushioned economically, how much of real life do you think they truly experience and understand?

My guess . . . not much. Now at this point, someone in their position could easily find himself believing he is superior to all those who have to pay for their tickets.

I don't blame these celebrities for being self-important. I can imagine that it is really hard to stay tethered in the real world when you live in HollyWorld, when you live the lifestyle that these people have to live.

Imagine your neighbor, your friend, a guy you hang out with, talk to and respect being . . . Marlon Brando. This is a guy who, I've read, has McDonald's literally throw the burgers over his fence, so he doesn't have to go to McDonald's himself. McDonald's *delivers* to Marlon Brando's house—but not to the door—they throw the burgers at him like he's some kind of zoo animal.

Hey, Marlon—what kind of Matrix are you living in? Here's an idea: take your limo to the drive-through. Go out from time to time and buy the hamburgers yourself. Or better yet, don't go at all, and lose some weight. Just meet some people and slow down on the Big Macs, Grimace.

So, it is no longer a question of How could they feel superior? It's "Could they believe everyone else thinks the way they do?" That their out-of-step opinions are actually the opinions of the majority?

Let me answer with a question: If you live in Malibu and you're isolated because of your celebrity, who are your friends?

Answer: others isolated by their celebrity status or money.

So you're sitting around at cocktail parties saying, "Ohhhh, well I think Tim Robbins and Susan Sarandon are *exactly* right."

Of course you do! You're hanging out with Barbra Streisand and Mike Farrell and when you see Susan Sarandon and Tim Robbins out—they're not out at the movie theater seeing real people—they're out at your Malibu beach house, Barbie!

Their job is to create a fantasy world, and they live in that fantasy world. In the film *My Favorite Year,* Peter O'Toole plays a hopeless drunk, an Errol Flynn character. In one scene he's up at the top of a building in New York, dead drunk, and he says, "I'm going to take this rope"—which is a fire hose—"and I'm going to throw it down a few floors to the balcony and shimmy down."

And Mark Linn-Baker, who plays the Mel Brooks character, stops him and says, "You can't just shimmy down a fire hose!" And O'Toole says, "Of course I can! I've been trained to climb mountains by Niblet!"

"Who's Niblet?"

"My Himalayan guide!"

"Your Himalayan guide?—that was in a *movie.* Niblet doesn't exist. You were trained to shimmy by a character. *That was a movie—this is real life!*"

Then, in one of my favorite lines, a perplexed Peter O'Toole queries, "What *is* the difference?"

He really doesn't know the difference. Nor do many "real life" Hollywood stars.

My Message to Hollywood

The citizens of HollyWorld also seem perplexed as to why, right after the War with Iraq, a Susan Sarandon TV movie

would come in something like 444th place on TV. They don't understand why people were rejecting them and not watching their movies. Let me see if I can break it down for them.

Okay, Martin Sheen. I love *West Wing*. Even though I'm a conservative, it's been a great escape for me on Wednesday nights.

I love to see how the other half thinks. God bless ya.

I am also a big fan of you, Martin Sheen, as an actor. But you know what? After I saw your face on TV talking about politics *as Martin Sheen* over and over again, you lost your effectiveness as an actor. You became Martin Sheen and not the president on the *West Wing* TV show.

The ultimate actor is an empty vessel, a blank canvas. You're supposed to be able to play any character and make us believe it. When we begin to see the actor and not the role you are playing, it destroys the illusion.

I no longer believe you as President Bartlett. I only see Martin Sheen, a Hollywood liberal with an agenda.

I also could no longer buy into the CBS Sunday night movie character played by poor little Susan Sarandon. You remember the one where she was some scientist down on the polar ice cap with cancer? All I could think was, "Man, I wish Susan Sarandon were *really* trapped on a polar ice cap." Not that I wish cancer on her or anything, but I remember thinking, "Trapped on the pole? Susan Sarandon? Sure."

So, why is it they are surprised that when they come and relentlessly speak out, they are no longer as effective as an actor or an actress? Oh, I'm sorry—that's politically incorrect of me. There are no actresses anymore. Everyone is an actor now.

It's like Adam Sandler or Jim Carrey trying to do a serious movie when we're used to seeing them play idiots. When these Hollywood actors come out and have opinions that are so far out of the mainstream, we no longer see anything but them in those roles, and it doesn't work.

And another thing: My not watching *West Wing* anymore isn't a "boycott." It isn't trying to take away your right to free speech. It is just me not being able to escape into a *West Wing* fantasy world, which I really want to enjoy, because all I keep seeing in my head is the fantasy world Martin Sheen lives in when the cameras are no longer rolling.

Here's what I would like to point out to Hollywood: Let's just be honest—you hate George Bush. And that's fine. I can understand that. You're the yin to my yang. But don't try to couch it in this "Oh, this war is wrong" bullcrap. Just come out and say it: "I hate George Bush. He was selected not elected."

Another thing, please don't call the man "stupid." He went to Yale and has an MBA from Harvard. I don't know about you, but I've been checking my walls, and I haven't seen my MBA from Harvard and I don't see my Yale diploma either. You don't get into those places if you're a big, fat dummy.

My irritation is that they're accusing George Bush of being stupid, and stupid people just don't make it at Harvard and Yale. Sure, you might get accepted because of Daddy's little CIA background—there may have been black choppers flying over Harvard, threatening the dean of admissions if George didn't get in—but I think the whole CIA agent thing would stop kicking in if George were failing test after test after test. That's what dummies do—they fail.

You want to talk about dummies? Let's look at the aca-
demic achievements of some of the Hollywood crowd:

Let's see . . . Barbra Streisand completed high school. Con-
grats on that, Babs.

Martin Sheen flunked an exam to enter the University of
Dayton. Sure, it's right up there with Harvard. But Dayton's
got the advantage of giving students an easy look at the Delco
radio plant.

Jessica Lange dropped out of college mid-freshman year.

Alec Baldwin dropped out of George Washington University. By the way, is he still packing his bags? I'm willing to
send the guy a freaking U-Haul truck.

Sean Penn: Who's a cute little high school grad? You are!

Susan Sarandon actually got a degree in drama from
Catholic University in Washington, D.C. Susan, congratula-
tions. You have an actual education from an actual university.

Ed Asner completed high school.

George Clooney dropped out of the University of Kentucky.

Michael Moore dropped out during his first year at the University of Michigan. But let's cut the Stay Puff Marshmallow
Man some slack—he was probably too racked with pain about
big business to study.

Mike Farrell completed high school.

Janeane Garofalo dropped out of college.

Yeah, and who's the big dumb dummy?

Name one of these actors who *completed* college, with a special exception made to my polar-ice-cap dream girl Susan
Sarandon.

> Knock, knock.
> Who's there?
> Orange.

In my perfect world, here's how *Thelma and Louise* really ends. Susan Sarandon, played by herself, drives the car over the cliff. No survivors. The end. Actually, that's the whole movie. It may be short, but *I'd* pay $7.50 to see it. Wouldn't you?

Oops. That's not very Christlike of me either, is it?

The point is not that everyone has to go to college to succeed or be smart, but it does help. I went to Yale University for one semester when I was thirty—I spent more time trying to find a parking space than I did in class. I wish I would have finished—I could guarantee I would be much more qualified to offer some of the opinions I spout every day. Not because of a piece of paper hanging on the wall, but I would be more qualified because a formal education helps to discipline the mind. The real benefit of college is not to be taught *what* to think but *how* to think.

Does anyone else find it interesting that you can't name the "dumb" Democrats? Name the "idiots" that were called "not smart enough" to have served in the White House? Dan Quayle, Ronald Reagan, George W. Bush. Right? Now name the liberals that have been labeled as dumb. No one.

Besides being a conservative, what kinds of qualifications do you need to be on the list of stupid people? How about

GPA? If you want to look at the record of George Bush versus Al Gore, George Bush had better grades than Al Gore did. Does that mean anything? Not really.

You can disagree with his politics, God bless you, but that's not really what's happening here. They're not arguing the politics. They're not arguing the policies. Maybe they can't go any deeper than, "Liberal good—Conservative bad!"

It seems to be almost a pattern: *If a politician is a Republican or a conservative, he must be stupid.*

Tempting as it might be, I am not going to play the same game. Not even for a million dollars.

> Regis: "Who is a big, fat dummy?"
> Me: "Michael Moore."
> Regis: "You still have all of your life lines.
> Do you want to call a friend?"
> Me: "No, I'm pretty sure it's [c]—Michael Moore."
> Regis: "Final answer?"
> Me: "Yes—[c]—Michael Moore—final answer."

To me it is not that Hollywood celebrities are stupid—it is that they are either being intellectually dishonest or naïve. They seem to really believe the lie of the Communist Party called "immiseration."

When Communist Russia figured out in the middle of the last century that the American workers would never "overthrow" the U.S. government, they had to change their strategy. Up until that time the slogans had been "workers unite," figuring that the ruling class would never share power. But an amazing and purely American thing happened. The Rockefellers, Gettys and Carnegies realized that it was in their best interest to close down the sweat shops. It wasn't an easy transition but it happened. The little guy *did* have a voice and through relatively peaceful means, he could change the way his world worked.

Now, the Communists faced a dilemma: If they couldn't count on the workers to rise up, who could stop the expansion of democracy? Who could they count on? They came up with two solutions: one we will discuss later in chapter 6, The Enemy Within. The other was immiseration.

It was a theory that the workers in America were part of the problem and not the solution. The problem was that American corporations—along with the full knowledge and support of their workers—were inflicting evil on the rest of the world, because we all were too darn greedy. The theory was that because we had much, they had none. Sound familiar? When you hear "What did we do to cause this?" or that you and I and Ronald McDonald are somehow responsible for the horrific living conditions in Africa, it's just more immiseration that started in Red Square as the way to destroy democracy.

It's as though those in HollyWorld believe that if American conservatives would just change their attitudes, Muslim extremists would vanish—as would hunger, poverty and racism. North Korea would open up all of their prisons and everyone would live happily every after.

What I find puzzling is that Hollywood and liberals don't

distrust government—they just distrust Republicans. They are fine taxing, spending and growing the monster that lives in the Beltway. When people claim that liberals hate America, or that they're anti-American, they are wrong. They just hate George W. Bush, Ronald Reagan and other conservatives. You wouldn't have heard those same "What did we do to deserve it?" lines coming out of Hollywood had September 11 happened during the Clinton years—unless they could have pinned it on Iran-Contra.

Government is good, it seems, unless it is in the hands of conservatives.

Tom Hanks and Jimmy Stewart:
The Good Celebrities

Tom Hanks is the ultimate celebrity in the Real America.

Tom, I don't know what you think about politics. I don't know who you voted for. I don't know what your stance is on the war on terror.

And I'm happy about that.

When we watch Tom Hanks on a deserted island for three hours, trying to make his way back to his FedEx job, we're watching not just the character on the screen. When we watch Tom Hanks on an island or in *Apollo 13,* we're also watching ourselves.

An actor like Tom Hanks is, in many ways, such a blank canvas that he almost becomes a mirror. We see pieces of ourselves in him. And then, beyond that, because of the characters that he chooses and the way he plays them, we see the "us" we strive to be in him: the guy who's just a little bit better than we are. That's why Tom Hanks is as powerful, as moving and as adored in America as he is.

He's the Jimmy Stewart of our generation.

Now I can tell you Jimmy Stewart would not have been the guy protesting against the war. He's not the guy who would've been making stump speeches about "selected not elected." Jimmy Stewart was above that. He was better than that. He was the big picture. He was goodness and compassion and the struggle of Everyman. And whether he was beating his kids with coat hangers—I don't care. I don't know. I don't want to know.

> Knock, knock.
> Who's there?
> Orange.

Mike Sweeney

Mike Sweeney is a guy in Kansas City who plays for the Royals. He could go and play anywhere. The people on his team at first thought that he was a fake, because he was too nice to everyone.

Mike Sweeney will look out onto the field and call out, "Hey, Bill and Sally, good to see you again!"

Now, who the heck are Bill and Sally? They're just two

fans in the stands. But Mike Sweeney actually remembers people who came to the game. He'll say, "Oh, yeah, Bill and Sally—they came to the game about six months ago. I met them here and I haven't seen them in the stands since then. It's good to see them again."

This guy has more than a great memory. He actually cares about the people who are coming to watch him play. He recognizes that the fans can spend their money on other things, and he's honored that they would spend their money to watch him. Beyond that, he's just a good guy. He could go and play baseball for anybody else.

He doesn't want to.

He likes his own town of Kansas City. He likes playing with the Royals. He thinks it's a good organization. It's not all about money—he's paid a lot of money, sure, but he's just playing ball.

Hey, big-bucks baseball players, do you hear that? For the love of Pete, do you recognize that you're just playing a *game?*

It's not just the celebrities in Hollywood who are the problem, it's also the celebrities in sports. I'm so sick of hearing players say, "Well, I'm not a role model."

Yes, you are, I'm sorry to break it to you, *but kids are watching you—just like you watched Hank Aaron.*

If you don't want people to watch you, then maybe you should play baseball for the Montreal Expos.

Do you remember being a kid and having a favorite player? Do you remember being a kid and watching that baseball game and thinking, "Ah, someday, maybe, I could pitch in the World Series."

Those players are important to our kids, just as they were to us. You tell me that Billy Crystal wasn't influenced by Mickey Mantle. Of course he was. Look at his movies—he was a Mickey Mantle nut. Kids look up to them, no matter how much the players don't want the kids to look up to them.

The problem is we have two kinds of celebrities: the kind of celebrities who say, "I'm just doing my job and I'm not a role model"—they usually turn out like Dennis Rodman. Or we have the celebrities who understand they're a role model—and behave like responsible citizens.

Now if you're John Rocker, and you want to let everybody know that white is better and that's just the way it is, well, then God bless you, but I'm going to boo you every time you come out on the field.

But you have a right to say it—*yada yada, yada . . .*

If you're an actor, just so you know, I may not buy into your character anymore when you're trying to be someone else. That's why when Tim Robbins comes out and says, "Hey! People are trying to hurt my freedom of speech by not going to my movie," two things come to mind. First, we aren't going to the movie because we can't see the character past you, and second, just like I don't want to watch John Rocker play baseball because he says things like "I don't want to ride the train with some queer with AIDS," I don't really want to spend my money on movies starring you. I don't want to help pay your salary. It's okay for you to have an opinion, and it's okay for you to make movies, but if I don't want to go to your baseball game or see your movie, that's called *my* freedom of speech.

I'm not "boycotting" or calling sponsors. I'm not pressing for a "black list" in your liberal world, even though there is a "black list" for us conservatives in my business. It is called the "no buy" list. Talk-show hosts get on this list when liberals want to shut them down. They begin letter-writing campaigns and national boycotts. So, many national sponsors just put certain shows on the "no buy" list to avoid the hassle.

To quote Tim Robbins, "There is a chill wind blowing across this nation as some try to silence the voices of others."

So say all you want, but understand that there are consequences to everything you say or do. There are consequences to your pocket, and there are consequences to society, because you are a role model.

My Note to Barbra Streisand

Dear Barbra,

I'm writing you this note because I know I will never get to meet you. You're just too big a celebrity. I also fear I might lose all my power to do good, because I believe you may just be my Kryptonite. So I'm going to pass this note on to you in the hope that you'll see it.

Here's my message: *You love big government, Barbra. I don't.*

You love those social programs the government

wants to give us. But the thing is, Barbra, you can *afford* to love big government. The rest of us can't. You see, Barbra, you have more money than God, or at least more money than the pope. However, for those of us who live on planet Earth and don't sleep in $300,000 Stickley beds, we'd like to be able to direct some of our money to places that *we* want. Such as our own families and businesses.

You, on the other hand, have so much capital that your family and dreams are set for generations. And yet you still have *more* money so now you can start foundations to help one-legged drug addicts buy new needles. When you're done funding that, you still have money. We don't.

Even if I wanted to help one-legged drug addicts, I couldn't, because after my family, tithing, business and taxes, I have nothing left. So I don't have the luxury of choosing how and who to help as you do.

But it seems that you believe it is the government's place to solve the world's problems: more taxes, more programs and more government, yet when you fail to add extra digits to your IRS check your actions expose you as a conservative.

Ms. Streisand—and the Ms. part makes me want to gag—if you really meant it, if you really believed what you were preaching, you would let Big Government decide how to spend your money, because your beloved

Big Government knows how to spend your money better than you do. Right?

It seems to me that you would not give your big donations to whomever you give them to—the Panda and Tofu Foudation or the White-Billed Cockatoo Conservation Society and the Let's All Walk to Work and Dispose of Our Cars Foundation. To remain consistent with your line of thought one would think that you would take all of that money and just write a check directly to the Internal Revenue Service so they could give it to the people and groups *they* thought deserved it.

So, go ahead, Barbra. Put your money where your mouth is. Write those seven-figure checks to the IRS, not to the Children Without Faces Fund.

Love and kisses,
Glenn

What Hollywood Doesn't Understand

It's important for Hollywood to understand that most conservatives, just like most liberals, are Americans through and through, and they understand that people have the right to speak out. They have the right to protest. They even have a right to differ on policy. They have a right to differ on principles.

No one of sound mind and reason is calling someone un-American for protesting or speaking out. There's nothing more American than that. It started with the Boston Tea Party.

God bless you, Hollywood, for speaking out.

But what you have to understand is that if you find yourself in the minority opinion, it's not because of some vast, right-wing or left-wing conspiracy. It's because you're out of step with what everybody else thinks.

You're not going to be rounded up in the middle of the night and taken to jail. *That's* what freedom of speech really means: that the government is not going to kick your door open in the middle of the night, even though, as we have already established, the president's dad probably still has connections to those people with black helicopters.

But they're not going to come and kick your door in. They're not going to haul you away and leave you to rot in jail, like people did in Saddam Hussein's world.

That doesn't happen in America.

But there is a price to pay for expressing your opinions.

Do you remember Sambo's? I think Sambo's restaurants have a right to exist, and they can have Little Black Sambo up on their signs and they can make "No Blacks Flapjacks" all they want.

But I'm not going to eat there.

The restaurants have a right to exist. The government shouldn't come in, kick their doors down and shut them down.

I have a right to express my freedom of association and speech by not ordering Sambo's flapjacks.

I have a right to express my freedom of association and speech by not watching Susan Sarandon trapped at the polar ice cap.

I have a right to express my freedom of association and speech by not going to Michael Moore movies or buying his books.

I have a right to express my freedom of association and speech by not watching Martin Sheen on *West Wing* anymore.

And I have a right to express my freedom of association and speech by throwing out all of my Barbra Streisand CDs. I'm not organizing a boycott or asking anybody to do it.

Because in the Real America, it is all about personal choice and the power of the individual.

Knock, knock.
Who's there?
Orange.
Orange who?
Orange you glad you're not a morbidly obese, violently grotesque, greasy, hair-covered, sweat-drenched Gila monster who is simultaneously both completely irrelevant to society and also a filthy, cancerous scourge on humanity, like Michael Moore.

CHAPTER 4

Everything You Need to Know About Partisan Politics

Blah blah blah **talking points** blah blah blah-blah-blah. Blah blah blah blah **diplomatic failures** blah blah-blah blah/blah/blah blah blah, "Blah blah blah blah blah blah blah blah." Blah blah blah blah blah blah:

- Blah blah blah blah **campaign finance reform.**
- Blah blah blah blah **Medicare and Social Security.**
- Blah blah blah blah **homeland security.**
- Blah blah blah blah blah blah blah blah blah blah blah blah blah blah blah blah blah blah blah blah blah blah blah blah blah blah **the American people.**

The **2000 election** blah blah blah, **Florida** blah blah blah **George W. Bush** blah blah blah blah blah blah blah blah blah **selected not elected.**

Blah blah **Al Gore** blah blah blah **demand a recount** blah blah blah blah **butterfly ballots.** Blah blah blah blah **hanging chads** blah blah blah blah **butterfly ballots** blah blah blah blah **Katherine Harris.** Blah blah blah blah blah blah blah blah **Jeb Bush.**

Blah blah blah blah **Bill Clinton** blah blah blah blah **impeached but not removed** Blah blah *blah blah* **Monica Lewinsky,** blah blah blah blah **blue dress;** blah blah blah blah **Linda Tripp.** Blah blah blah blah **Slick Willie** blah blah blah blah **Hillary Clinton** blah blah blah blah **universal health care.** Blah blah blah blah **no child left behind.** Blah blah blah blah blah blah blah blah blah blah blah blah **vast right-wing conspiracy.**

***Note: blah, blah blah.

Blah blah blah blah **big business,** blah blah blah blah **big oil,** blah blah blah blah **big tobacco,** blah blah blah blah **racist warmongers. Seventy-two percent of** blah, blah blah blah blah, **and 19 percent of** blah. Blah?? **Where's the** blah? Blah blah blah blah **tax cuts for the rich only,** blah blah blah blah **disenfranchised,** blah blah blah blah **being silenced,** blah blah blah blah **the wealthiest 1 percent.**

Blah blah blah blah **Clarence Thomas,** blah blah blah blah **Anita Hill,** blah blah blah blah **modern-day lynching,** blah blah blah blah **nutty and slutty.** Blah blah blah blah **liberal elitist,** blah blah blah blah **right-wing extremists,** blah blah blah blah **party of the little people.**

Blah blah blah and the blah.

1. Blah blah and blah.
2. Blah the blah **before the** blah **has too much** blah.
3. Blah **it, then** blah **the** blah **over the** blah **AND** blah—under-standing that blah **is greater than** blah.
4. **Always remember** . . . blah.

Blah blah blah blah **Janet Reno,** blah blah blah blah **Elian Gonzalez,** blah blah blah blah **Waco.** Blah blah blah **Enron,** blah blah blah blah **Global Crossing,** blah blah blah blah **Iran-Contra,** blah blah blah blah **Chappaquiddick.**

Blah blah blah blah **flag-waving zealots,** blah blah blah blah **anti-American,** blah blah blah blah **corporate overlord,** blah blah blah blah **Zionist masters.**

Blah blah blah blah **Tom Daschle,** blah blah blah blah blah blah blah blah **Sponge Bob Square Pants,** blah blah blah blah blah **Trent Lott! Trent Lott!**

Blah blah blah blah blah:

   Rep. Blah (R-Ohio): Blah blah blah.

   Rep. Blah (D-South Dakota): No, blah blah blah blah-blah.

   Rep. Blah (R-Ohio): Wrong. Blah blah blah, **then** blah blah buh blah-blah.

   Rep. Blah (D-South Dakota): Clearly, blah blah blah **has a** blahing **agenda of** blah **and** blah.

> Rep. Blah (R-Ohio): Oh, yeah, well—BLAH!!
>
> Rep. Blah (D-South Dakota): Me BLAH?—NO—
> YOU BLAH!!
>
> Rep. Blah (R-Ohio): BLAH OFF YOU BLAH-IN'
> BLAH!
>
> Rep. Blah (D-South Dakota): BLAH YOU!
>
> Rep. Blah (R-Ohio): BLAH YOU TIMES TWO!!!

Blah blah blah blah **scorched-earth policy,** blah blah blah blah **destroying the environment,** blah blah blah blah **tree-hugging liberal.**

Blah blah blah blah **Watergate,** blah blah blah blah **Travelgate,** blah blah blah blah blah blah blah blah **hate speech** blah blah blah. Blah. Blah blah blah (blah blah blah blah blah blah blah blah) blah blah blah blah blah blah blah **it's the economy, stupid.** Blah blah blah blah blah **aspirin factory** blah blah blah blah. Buh-blabba blah blah blah blah blah blah blah blah blah-blabberty blah "**jingoistic** blah blah." Blah blah blah blah blah-ma blah-ma ding dong, blah blah blah blah blah blah **pay raise.** Booka-blabba ah blab buh-blah blah blah blah blakula blah blah blah & blah blah blah blah binkie-blah. Boompah-loompah blah blah blah blah blah blah blah blah blah blah **WMD? What did** blah **know and when did** blah **know** blah?? Blah blah blah blah blah **boo-berry** blah blah blah. Blah blah blah. Blah blah blah blah blah blah **sand-ridden rat hole.**

In conclusion, blah blah blah blah blah—blah blah blah—

blah blah blah blah blah **"b to the l-a-h"** blah blah. **Barnacles!**
Blah blah blah blah blah blah blah blah bloopty-bloop blah
blah blah blah blah blah blah blah blah blah blahhhhhhhhhe.
(The e is silent.) Blah blah blah, blah blah blah blah, **and I ask
you—can you find the one time in this chapter that** blah **is
spelled backward? If so, email me at** blahblahblah@blah.blah.

Blah, blah, blah . . . **and God bless the United** Blah **of**
Ameri-blah.

CHAPTER 5

Hitler and Jesus Had One Thing in Common

Once the statue of Saddam Hussein was pulled down in Baghdad, everyone in America decided the War with Iraq was over. Everyone went back to thinking about other things. Everyone went back to sleep.

And then the terrorist bombings started up again—in Israel, in Saudi Arabia, in Morocco. As soon as people started talking about peace, the bombings started again. Gee, maybe the war was not really over. Maybe it was just beginning.

Let's review. We learned three lessons in Vietnam: The first was that the Jane Fondas of the world *do* make a difference. We choose as a nation which direction we go in: Do we spit on our marines when they come back? Do we call them "baby killers"? Or do we stand behind them? This time around most Americans made a different choice than did John Cougar Mellencamp, Sheryl Crow and Natalie Maines. We asked, "Can't we unite behind them, disagreeing with the policies perhaps, but standing behind the men and women of our armed forces once hostilities began?"

I stood shoulder to shoulder with many who questioned the timing of the war at the Rallies for America. Once our troops were in harm's way, we closed ranks behind them. Some who questioned President Bush's policy did support the troops; however, that can't be said for all of them. One example stands out: a sign held by a protestor in New York that read: I SUP-PORT THE TROOPS AS SOON AS THEY START SHOOTING THEIR OFFI-CERS. That's the path we ran down in the 1960s, the lesson we learned after Vietnam.

That's why the Rallies for America were so important. That's why hundreds of thousands of people came out to the rallies. That's why, when asked for a single dollar, 443,000 people sent me 443,000 one-dollar bills to support the USO and fund the Rally for America.

It wasn't that everybody was so gung-ho to invade Iraq and free the Iraqis. What Americans were feeling at the time was, "I am not sure that the timing is just right, but I *do know* that I don't want to be part of an America that creates another gen-eration of veterans who question themselves and wonder, 'Am I a Baby Killer?' "

So when Hollywood started to go down that 1960s path, when the UN started to go down that path, when Commu-nists started to go down that path, something had to be done in response. I know it sounds ridiculous in this day and age to talk about Communists, but when the voices lead by Interna-tional A.N.S.W.E.R. in America and Europe started to tear

America apart—and started to tear our soldiers apart—that's when the average person in the Real America said, "No. Not this time. Not again."

That was maybe the most important lesson of Vietnam: how to treat our armed forces, our brave, heroic young men and women.

One Vet's Story: Mike and His Dog

Years ago I worked with a guy—I'll just call him Mike—at a small Top 40 radio station. I was a nineteen-year-old kid, programming an FM show, and Mike was on the oldies AM station. He was a washed-up, angry alcoholic, and usually there wasn't even anybody listening to him.

Mike used to bring his Rottweiler to work—a giant Rottweiler, and angrier than Mike. Needless to say, Mike and his dog weren't very popular. He didn't seem to have any friends. Nobody really liked Mike . . . including Mike.

But no one at the station ever said anything critical about Mike or his show, because, well, there was this giant, angry Rottweiler sitting there next to him. So he was an absolutely friendless, isolated, mean, twisted and angry man, the orneriest SOB I have ever met.

And did I mention the Rottweiler?

I did my show in one studio, Mike did his show in the other, across the soundproof glass. He was facing me, and I was facing him. We did our shows five days a week, four hours a day, looking at each other, although I couldn't hear him and he couldn't hear me. We could see each other through the sound-proof glass.

Now in radio, good hosts always imagine they are talking to one person, whether that person is in a car or at home or at an office in a cubicle.

For me, that person was Mike. He couldn't hear me, but I was talking directly to him.

And for those few months, without thinking about it, I looked in Mike's eyes for almost four hours a day, and it got so that I could tell that, underneath it all, he was a decent, humble, gracious, man. A gentle man—not a gentleman, but a gentle man. Not the angry alcoholic with the big dog the rest of the world saw.

Now just before I decided that I wanted to be his friend, and right before he decided that he wanted me to be his friend, Mike spent a weekend alone in his apartment with the Rottweiler, and a shotgun in his mouth.

He told me later that he spent that weekend praying for the strength to pull the trigger. He told me that he literally spent most of the weekend with the gun in his mouth, going from crying to praying to getting angry again, just wanting to pull the trigger, just wanting the pain to end. But somehow he just couldn't do it.

The thing that saved his life was that Rottweiler.

Every time Mike was about to pull the trigger, he would look over at that Rottweiler, and he would see that dog's eyes—

Now I know what you're thinking, "Awwww, you know the way that dogs look at you . . . they're so friendly and they feel such unconditional love. . . ."

Not Mike's Rottweiler.

Every time Mike was about to pull the trigger, he would look into that dog's eyes and he would hear the dog think, "Go ahead, pull it. But in three days, when nobody comes to check on you because you're a friendless loser, I'll be hungry. *And I will eat you.*"

Mike didn't want to be eaten by his dog. *That's* what saved his life.

So we became friends. And Mike is one of the greatest men I have ever met, one of the nicest. He became one of my greatest friends.

Part of what happened to make Mike bitter was Vietnam.

Mike now takes responsibility for his life, as all good Real Americans do. He no longer blames his turmoil on Vietnam. But what happened was that Mike served his country proudly and well in Special Forces, which means that it was his job to do unspeakable things. Special Forces does the kinds of jobs that have to be done in a war, but you and I don't want to hear about. Those jobs were Mike's specialty.

So Mike came back from Vietnam a highly trained professional. But he came back to a country that was spitting on those professionals, spitting on guys who have more bravery in their little fingers than I have in my entire body. Remember, I'm the guy in *Saving Private Ryan,* who is crying up in a corner at the top of the stairs, unable even to point my gun, let alone shoot it.

In Special Forces, Mike was the guy who would be dropped behind enemy lines, where he would live among the villagers, without the villagers ever knowing, waiting for the one guy they were looking for, so Mike could shoot and kill him then get back out, all by himself.

But the thing he said to me that was the most devastating was simply, "I was good at my job." That's what got to him: "I was very good at my job, Glenn, and my job was to kill people."

You can't train people to assassinate people and then, when they come back, tell them, "You're a worthless baby killer, and you did it for no reason."

Mike came back to a country where, when he went on a job interview, someone once looked at his resume and said, "Oh, I see here that you were in Vietnam," to which Mike replied, "Yes, sir. I was."

Mike was proud of it. "Yes, *sir,* I was!" He was a professional.

"Oh . . . that's too bad," the interviewer said.

Mike was looked down upon. His service was made to be much less than a heroic or honorable act. Mike was made to feel ashamed of what he had done.

It took Mike many years to recover from that.

How many Mikes never recovered?

On a side note, as I was working with Mike on how to win friends and influence people, I gave him two pieces of advice. One, stop bringing the dog to work. Two, stop telling people that you were good at killing people. There are simply better ways of starting off conversations.

Mike was one reason why I felt so strongly—and I think that the rest of America felt just as strongly—about standing behind our troops in the War with Iraq.

Because we all know a Mike. And we didn't want to create any more guys who would have to spend forty years trying to find the answer—whether the answer was death at the bottom of a bottle or at the other end of a shotgun.

I invited Mike to the Vietnam War Memorial years ago. He had never been, and he didn't want to go. He finally worked up enough courage and asked me to take him. Here's one of the bravest, strongest men I know, and he was absolutely incapacitated at the wall. He collapsed and felt so many names that I'll never forget it, watching him put his fingers in each letter of each name he knew, sobbing beyond belief. This is a big guy—he put an arm around me and an arm around my wife and we walked him back to the car.

Mike let go of Vietnam that day. A lot of his buddies didn't make it.

It's All About the Village

The second most important lesson we learned in Vietnam was that it's all about the village. We weren't really fighting an army in Vietnam, just as we weren't really fighting an army in the Middle East. We go over to these places, this giant superpower, and we want to fight and crush an army in the conventional way. But that wasn't what was happening in Vietnam. They were fighting a guerilla war in the jungles and, more important, in the villages.

We lost Vietnam because we sent our army to fight their

army and there was no real army to fight. That wasn't where the danger was. The danger was in the villages.

By the time we got to Vietnam, the Communists had already gone into the villages and fed the villagers and befriended them and taken care of them. They said to them, "Communism is good. Why don't you give it a try?" The villages then became the eyes and ears of the Communists, their first line of real defense.

We didn't understand that, because we weren't hungry in the 1960s. We didn't listen to the propaganda, we didn't take it seriously, because we already knew that Communism didn't work. We knew that there was nothing to it, except oppression of the human spirit. Communism wasn't neat. The Vietnamese were hungrier than we were. They wanted a change. They wanted an answer. They needed to believe that Communism was a solution to their problems.

It all goes back to the comparison between Jesus and Hitler. What Jesus and Hitler had in common was they both looked at people who had problems and said, "I have the solution. Come and follow me." Both offered bread to the masses, but Jesus also offered spiritual sustenance.

When people are hungry, spiritually or physically, they will follow. When someone looks them in the eye and convincingly says, "I have an answer," they will follow. That's what the Communists did to the Vietnamese. That's what the Taliban did to the Afghans. That's how Hamas has their fingers around the throats of the Palestinians. They feed them and tell them they can solve their problems.

We must go into the villages and find out what the terror-

ists are feeding the Islamic community here in America. What is it that Muslims are so hungry for that they will eat it from the hands of Al Qaeda?

We now need to apply the second lesson: We're not fighting an army in the war against terrorism. Nor are we fighting an army in Afghanistan or in Iraq. We have to go in and look at the villages and the villagers.

And the villages this time are not just in foreign lands. They're not just in the jungle.

The villages this time are Buffalo, New York. They're Detroit, Michigan. They're San Diego, California, or Phoenix, Arizona, or South Florida, where the hijackers from 9/11 came. Those are the villages in America, and some in the Islamic community are sheltering the terrorists. What America must understand is that all future wars will be asymmetrical. Our military is too big and powerful to be fought conventionally. The coming military conflicts will be fought in the streets by the villagers.

Most members of the American Islamic community refuse to call the terrorists "friend," and rightly so. But they also refuse to call them "foe." This is a war that we have to fight in the village, alongside the villagers. That doesn't mean that we fight Islam, but it does mean that Muslims have to fight alongside us. More important, they need to *want* to fight alongside us.

The place to start is to drop the phrase "Yes, terrorism is bad, but . . ." from your vocabulary and clearly take a stand by calling the terrorists everyone's foes.

The Third Lesson

Look what happened in Cambodia. The Cambodians said, "Once we get these evil Americans out of here, everything is going to be sweet. All of our problems will be solved."

And we bought into that "evil American" stuff here at home: "Oh, look . . . that poor little girl is running down the street naked . . . we can't do that to her . . . what are we trying to do these people? We're killing them! Let's go."

But as soon as the Americans left the region, the Cambodians turned on the Cambodians. The Khmer Rouge said to the Cambodians, "You're not Cambodian *enough*."

And then they conducted a reign of terror worse than anything that had come to Cambodia before.

On the bright side, Hollywood, the home of some of the people who got America to turn against the Vietnam war, actually had the opportunity to make millions of dollars and win some of those fancy gold statues on a movie about that wacky Pol Pot guy called *The Killing Fields*. Jane Fonda—America thanks you, and the dead Cambodians thank you.

Note to Islam: If you don't turn on these terrorists, you're going to learn the lesson of Cambodia the hard way. If you don't recognize that the terrorists are not your friends, if you allow them to destroy America, then once this foe is removed, you are next in line. That's when they will turn on you and say, "You're not Muslim *enough*." And who will be left to make a gold-statue-winning movie about you?

Maybe the French? Sure, and maybe Jerry Lewis can play you.

At a Talk-Show Convention

Last spring, I had to speak at a talk-show convention. There's nothing more agonizing than a group of talk-show people getting together to talk about talk shows.

You think your head's going to explode when you listen to the news? Imagine being in a roomful of 250 people who all think they have the answer and need about forty-five minutes each to explain it, quoting intricate tax code, using six-syllable words and each trying to out-Republican the other.

I sat on this panel, and it was the weekend *The Matrix* sequel opened. The moderator said, "Panel, isn't this an *exciting* time to be in talk radio? I mean look at the things that are going on: The president is trying to pass his tax plan, the Democrats are lining up to kick off their presidential campaigns, and there is a battle in the Senate over prescription drugs. . . . Isn't this *the* most exciting time to be in talk radio? Glenn—wouldn't you agree?"

And I said, "Well, yes, but not for any of the reasons you just outlined."

What an excruciating array of topics! When he was talking about politics, tax plans, campaigns and Grandpa's Lipitor, I was thinking, "Honestly, if I could take my belt off now and throw it around my neck, is there a place I could hang myself?"

Does anybody want to hang out with anybody who is excited by that collection of Jack Kevorkian, auto-suicidal CSPAN material? "Hey Bill, I know we're having a ton of fun talking about partisan politics now, but whaddya say about coming over Friday night and watching *Schindler's List!*"

So I said, "Actually, Steve"—we'll call him Steve—"what I talked about this week was *The Matrix*—the special effects, the action, and the chicks in the rubber suits. When I wanted to pretend I was smart, I let Jim Dingle peel another layer off this onion and talk about how scientists are now saying that *The Matrix* may soon be a reality through nanobot technology.

"I know it sounds totally insane, but this technology is already starting to shape up. The technology of a CAT scan is not good enough. We need to be able to see how the brain works from inside, so the Defense Department is working on nanobot technology, so they can shoot it into your brain or into your body and then those nanobots will beam images outside of your body into a computer. And did I mention the chicks in rubber suits?

"Now imagine our children's virtual reality with nanobot technology implanted in their visual cortex. You'll now log on-line by looking at a screen that isn't there, just like in the movie.

"Steve, this week wasn't about partisan politics or Hillary Clinton's book. It wasn't about long speeches, liberals or Lipitor. It was about a *movie* and a *rubber suit.* It was about what real people outside smoke-filled Washington think tanks were actually talking about."

"Fascinating stuff I'm sure to you, Glenn. But who's running for the Democratic presidential nomination a year and a half before the election? That is the kind of information people *need* to know." Please—somebody hand me that belt.

Here's what happened: The talk-show people on the panel all turned on me and started to tell me how we had a "respon-

sibility" to "teach" our listeners how "important" those Democratic primaries really are.

It's that high-and-mighty, self-absorbed, self-important nonsense that makes me want to kill every talk-show host in America.

And I'm not alone.

Talk-show hosts in America, look out. The American public is about to pick up a torch and a pitchfork and come looking for you.

But here's the interesting thing: Only the talk-show hosts on the *panel*—the ones who could hear their own voices—were interested in the partisan politics. The rest of the talk-show people in the audience? Well, you could see their eyes glazing over.

If you can't interest a roomful of talk-show hosts in partisan politics, you certainly can't get somebody who lives in Omaha, Nebraska, and works at the Dunkin' Donuts to listen to it.

Left and Right Wing Tips

Politics in general all comes down to two things: a left-wing-tip shoe and a right-wing-tip shoe.

You know them: these guys in their blue suits, wearing the wing-tip shoes and red ties—the ones who wake up and think, "Is this a red-tie day or a blue-tie day?" They have silver hair and bright smiles that smile at you, no matter what they're saying—unless you've just lost somebody, in which case they look at you with "great compassion." See, if you've lost somebody, they don't shake your hand with just one hand, they make sure they shake your hand firmly with one hand while they put their other hand behind your elbow, because it "brings you closer in to them."

What a bunch of plastic people. This is not the Real America.

And that's why you can't get people in America to show up to vote! Because they're not voting on anything they care about, anything they think really makes a difference. The Real Americans believe that politics nowadays is not real. It's all plastic done by plastic people. They don't think politicians actually get anything done. They don't think politics in Washington actually works. And they don't think that they can affect anything.

They're right on all of those points, except the last one.

Politics is all hogwash from the get-go, but you *can* affect things.

You know this is true about partisan politics, you know this is the way America feels, because more people voted for Ruben Studdard on *American Idol* than voted in the 2000 election.

Now, I personally believe that Ruben was selected not elected . . . but that's for another book.

People will turn on television and vote for contestants. What does that say about politics? They *trust* television. They want to get involved in television shows, when really, what is a television show? It's image. It's lip enhancements, boob jobs and frosted hair.

It's nothing but a giant lie!

But they still want to vote for the American Idol! Why? Be-

cause that's more real than the guys with the silver hair and the wing-tip shoes.

If Ray Romano would run for president, he would win. Why? Because he is a regular guy. But once he got to Washington, he would be sucked in by the same cynical party-line vacuum as everyone else.

And within about a month, he'd probably be wearing a blue suit with a red tie and those wing-tip shoes—and nobody would care about him ever again.

And if he were elected as Ray Romano and decided not to sell out, he'd be exiled to cochair a committee with Sonny Bono's wife and the wife of the dead guy who beat John Ashcroft.

So he'd have to start to play the game. He'd have to start to get involved in partisan politics.

But by playing the game, he'd become inconsequential to us, he'd become part of the problem, not part of the solution.

Our founding fathers had this down: The solution lies in the home, in the heartland, with the people—not with the people in Washington.

Unfortunately, in this society, no one believes you can be an actual person *and* go to Washington.

Why do you think people voted for Jesse Ventura?

Was that not the most surreal moment in American politics? The reason he was elected was that he said what he meant and he meant what he said. He might have been a professional wrestler, he might have been a showman, he might have even been a clown to many people, but he actually said what he believed, damn the consequences. He didn't care.

We need more politicians who step forward and say, "You

know what? I don't need this job that bad—I don't *want* this job that bad, and if you don't like me, I'll go back to making millions of dollars as a professional wrestler." When we get politicians who really don't care about the trappings of power, we'll be set.

Does Hillary Clinton Wear Wing Tips?

No. Hillary Clinton does not wear wing tips.

Hillary Clinton *is* a wing tip.

Hillary Clinton is a pair of wing tips in a pants suit.

Hillary Clinton fully embodies everything that is wrong with politicians today. She fully embodies everything I despise about politics. I don't believe she's real on any level.

Hillary had an opportunity, a place in time that very few people ever encounter: That time was when her husband was lying his face off and the blue dress was found. She had an opportunity—not to throw his clothes out onto the lawn of the White House—but to address the American people, in a dignified manner, and say:

What Hillary Should Have Said

My fellow Americans:

I believe in the president of the United States.

I believe in the presidency, as well as this particular president.

He has some grand ideas and he's a brilliant man.

However, as a human he has some real lackluster qualities.

I appreciate that, and we have struggled as man and wife for years.

However, as he has responsibilities, not only to our marriage but also to his position, we have a responsibility to the people of the United States of America. Like it or not, we are role models. It's not just about the economy. It's about so much more.

With that in mind, I support the president.

But I can no longer support this man as my husband at this time.

So I will be removing myself from the White House.

Whether Bill and I work this through, or whether Bill and I remain married, I don't know.

I know that both of us plan to work through it, but no woman should ever be treated as I have been treated and no woman should be humiliated as I have been humiliated.

I went on national television and talked about a vast right-wing conspiracy. Why? Because my husband was lying to me—and he knew it! He used me to help get him out of it. That's unacceptable. A spouse must be treated with respect and dignity.

I may be leaving the White House, but I am not leaving my president. He will always be that; however,

> at this time I'm not sure he will remain my husband.
> This will be the last time I address this issue.
> Thank you for your prayers and support.

If Hillary Clinton had said that, she most likely would have destroyed Bill's career, but she could easily have been elected president in 2000 or 2004. Because people would at least have had respect for her. They would have said, "Now, here's a woman who won't stoop to anything just for power."

That's what Hillary Clinton is missing. Her whole life is politics. She's willing to be beyond humiliated so she can hold on to power.

Anyone who wants power that much, I don't want in Washington, D.C.

Not to mention, she's only in office because of Rudy Giuliani's prostate, which is another place I don't want to be.

With that being said, I still wouldn't have voted for her in 2000 or 2004, because her politics are upside down. She is, when all is said and done, a socialist.

Hey, here's an idea: *Socialism doesn't work*. Check the headlines from the past forty years, Hillary.

Now let's talk about Bill.

Hey, right-wing zealots—get over Bill Clinton. He's a part of our past. Move on with your life.

He is that ugly woman you woke up with, after that Saturday night when you got drunk beyond belief, the bar was starting to close, and you thought, "Well, what the heck—I want to go home with *somebody*."

That was Bill Clinton. That was the 1990s. He looked great at the time to almost 40 percent of us.

I don't know what we as a society were drinking, but it seemed many of us just wanted to bring him home.

We finally woke up after September 11, when Hillary Clinton walked onstage at that New York memorial to the police and firefighters and they booed her.

Actually, they weren't booing her. They were booing themselves and us. That was the moment when we woke up and rolled over in bed and saw what we had been sleeping with. We were sober, and it was the light of day. It was our collective "Coyote Moment." We woke up and realized that our arm was underneath the Clintons', and we'd rather chew it off to get out than risk waking them.

Hillary Clinton wasn't booed because of who she is. She couldn't have been. She hadn't changed. She hadn't done anything different. *We* changed after 9/11, and we didn't like ourselves for it. And we blamed it on them.

Don't blame it on the Clintons anymore. It wasn't the Clintons' fault.

Who didn't know what we were getting when we elected them? Come on, be honest, the only reason we left the bar with these two is because we were liquored up on the economy. For the love of Pete, for the first time in American history, we knowingly engaged in a presidential three-way. Now, no matter how much we shower, we can't get clean.

It's just like the people who blame Hollywood for violence because of the movies. "Look at all the horrible movies they're putting out! It's horrible! The horrifying horribility of it all is horrific." They're not putting out movies and then jamming them down our throats. During the Clinton era, Mark Wahlberg didn't drag you to *Boogie Nights*. Hollywood makes the films, and then you have the choice: "Am I putting my forty-seven-fifty down to see this movie or not?"

It's the same thing with the Clintons: They were just giving us what we wanted. And what we wanted was for our insatiable thirst for money to be satisfied. We were all about greed in the 1990s.

It *was* about the economy, stupid. It all boiled down to that in the end. Everything anybody ever said bad about America was true during that time: "It's all about business. It's all about oil. It's all about money. It's all about big corporations." Well, apparently it was. During the Clinton era, it was only about "How can I make more money?"

It *was* the economy, and we were stupid.

Don't hate Bill Clinton. He's a sad pathetic little guy. Think about it: Here's the guy who was the most powerful man in the world, and because he was such a slime ball, the only mark he's going to be remembered leaving is the one on a tarp of a cocktail dress. He's almost a joke or a parody of himself. I feel bad for Bill Clinton.

But he's part of our past, so let's move on.

Before we do, a lot of conservatives I know originally thought that there was a possibility that Bill Clinton must be the Antichrist. After all, he loves the UN, and you just know

he wants to be the secretary general someday—a "Left Behind" earmark of the Antichrist.

But let me tell you something: The Devil ain't that stupid. Bill Clinton is far too obvious a choice for the Antichrist.

Now, Hillary, on the other hand . . .

Me and Joe Lieberman

Sometimes, it is very frustrating for conservatives to listen to my program. I'm just not your stereotypical conservative. For instance, I am staunchly pro-life, and I'm also against the death penalty. Both of these are relatively new positions for me.

Confused yet, conservatives? How about this? I am a guy who worships the heart, the action and the intellect of Ronald Reagan. I voted for George Bush (41) and GWB.

I also voted for Joe Lieberman.

When I lived in Connecticut, I voted for Joe Lieberman because I trusted him. I believed him. I voted for him because he believes in responsibility exactly the way I believe in responsibility. He believes that corporations, Hollywood, as well as the individual, have rights, but they also have responsibilities.

I know Joe very well. Well, we're not buddies or anything, not like we're out buying yarmulkes together. But Joe is responsible for my being accepted at Yale. He wrote a recommendation for me, and I attended Yale University.

In getting to know Joe, I always told him that he was actually a conservative in the wrong party. We agreed on most principles, but we also disagreed on many of his policies. But the one thing I knew about Joe Lieberman was that he would say one thing to my face only to turn around and say *the exact same thing* behind my back.

He truly was a man of honor.

I say "was" because my relationship with Joe Lieberman fell apart during the Clinton/Lewinsky scandal. I told him that there were times when one man can make a difference, when one man can change the course of a whole nation. During the impeachment process, he was that man. I knew what he stood for, I knew what he believed in, and he certainly didn't stand for a scumbag being in the Oval Office. It goes against everything in him. Joe rails against Hollywood, Joe cries out for morals and values and the American family, and Joe's right on all those topics.

He came into my studio right before the impeachment vote, and I said, "Joe, I know you. I know your values. I went out and bought a book for you this weekend. Because the country is at a turning point and you can make the difference. I got you a copy of *Profiles in Courage*. I reread it this weekend and I think maybe you should read it again before the vote."

And I think he was a little offended—in fact, I know he was offended. He pushed the book back across the table toward me and said, "Glenn, I've read it."

So I pushed the book back and said, "I know you have, Joe, but maybe you should read it again. Because you're standing at a place where very few men ever get the opportunity to stand."

My friend Joe Lieberman pushed the book one final time, back across the table, and that was the last time we ever spoke.

As you probably remember, Joe Lieberman didn't take that point of history and change the course of America. I believe that he sold out his values—for what, I'll never know. One could guess, but it would remain just that . . . a guess.

But it's kind of like the National Organization for Women. They lost every bit of credibility they had with me—and it wasn't very much to begin with—because they accepted Bill Clinton, saying he was "better than the alternative." They hammered Clarence Thomas over a joke about a pubic hair on a Coke can. But here's a fifty-some-year-old guy who's making it with a twenty-year-old intern in the Oval Office—you want to talk about a guy abusing his power? That's the quintessential case, but they didn't want to hear about it. Why? Because they're a sham. It was really only about politics and power and money. So they embraced Bill Clinton because they just didn't want a Republican in office. Coincidently, the NOW organization received its first-ever government funding in LA at the height of the Clinton/Lewinsky scandal. (Read Tammy Bruce's book *The New Thought Police*.)

I don't want a president who's just better than the alternative. I want *the best*. But so many people *settled* for Bill Clinton.

I don't know why Joe Lieberman decided to settle, but he did. I voted for Joe Lieberman because he's the kind of guy who doesn't wear wing-tip shoes.

Then, in the 2000 election, Joe morphed into something I couldn't even recognize. I thought there was chance that Joe Lieberman could bring Al Gore into humanity. Al Gore is clearly some kind of Disney animatronic. If Al Gore had won the Florida election, the biggest winner would have been Disney. Because Al Gore could have gone directly to the Hall of Presidents and moved in, and then they wouldn't have had to spend any money on new electronics.

Maybe in 2000 Joe was just doing the VP dance, but I remember a better Joe Lieberman, a Joe Lieberman who would never have shirked his responsibility to the American people, to the ideals and the principles that we are supposed to stand for.

I remember a Joe Lieberman who stood for the Real America.

Socialism Is Exactly the Way We Should Live . . .

Socialism, in many ways, is exactly the way we should live, except I should be able to *freely* give my money to others. I shouldn't have my money forcibly taken from me and given to the government, so that *they* can decide what should be done with it.

In the Real America, we would all make as much money as we could possibly make, but then we'd only take what we need and we'd share the rest of it. Government can't do that. Only God can do that. Only spirituality can do that.

But socialism robs people of choice. And that is why socialism is evil.

One of the worst things that ever happened to America was Joseph McCarthy—and not for the reasons that everybody else thinks that Joseph McCarthy was a nightmare. I give you

that Joseph McCarthy was an out-and-out nightmare for all the reasons everybody thinks, but it goes much deeper than that.

Joseph McCarthy made cries of communism a joke. He makes the cries of socialism a joke. Nowadays when you say, "Um, you know, So-and-So is a Socialist," everybody laughs. It's like calling someone a witch, or a pirate. It just doesn't have any meaning anymore. "Oh no, he's a Socialist! So what?"

In the same way, Al Sharpton makes cries of racism a joke.

Keep it up, Al. You really want to hurt the cause of the African-Americans? Keep crying racism, because nobody will pay attention to you. When they hear it, it will become a joke, and they will laugh. Quite honestly, Al, the way they're laughing at your hair now.

So Joseph McCarthy had his witch-hunt in the 1950s, and he tried to find all the Socialists, all the commies, all the pinkos, and you know what? Some of them really existed. But the lasting repercussion of this is that nobody is afraid of socialism, nobody thinks communism is a bad thing.

Communism is all about power and manipulation. Socialism is all about telling people "You can't do it alone. You need big government to help you."

Tell me where the government doesn't screw up every time. Tell me a great government program. During the War with Iraq, I thought, "Well, maybe the military? Who does military better than the United States government?"

A few weeks later I opened up the paper and saw that the Pentagon was missing—catch this—one trillion dollars.

How is that possible? "Gee, where did I put that trillion dollars? Did I leave it in my jacket? Did I send it to the cleaners?"

How do you lose a trillion dollars? So tell me the thing the government does better than anyone else?

Highways, maybe. (By the way, everything you've read so far has been written while I sit in traffic on I-76 outside of Philadelphia.)

But socialism is big government's answer to compassion: a government-sponsored system of compassion.

Compassion shouldn't come from the government. In the Real America, compassion will come from the heart.

CHAPTER 6

The Enemy Within

A few years back I found, buried in the Congressional Record, something that a Florida congressman, Albert Herlong, Jr., submitted back in the mid 1960s. It was the "Communist Goals of 1963," a list of steps they needed to take to dismantle our way of life.

At a time when Americans are looking toward the destruction that can come our way from overseas in the form of a commercial airliner or a crop duster, I would like to resubmit these to the American people.

If I were on Al Qaeda's advisory board and I were asked, "How do we defeat America?" I would respond, "We cannot. They must defeat themselves." This was the understanding of the Communist Party at the height of the Cold War. As we watch for the enemy at our gates, realize that he may already be here. And he may have arrived in a Trojan horse called "liberalism."

As you read these, check off how many of them have already been accomplished. Not necessarily by the "Communists," but by liberals, special-interest groups, the ACLU and us.

Keep in mind, this was the list drafted to help destroy America.

1963 Communist Goals

1. US acceptance of coexistence as the only alternative to atomic war.

2. US willingness to capitulate in preference to engaging in atomic war.

3. Develop the illusion that total disarmament by the US would be a demonstration of "moral strength."

4. Permit free trade between all nations regardless of Communist affiliation and regardless of whether or not items could be used for war.

5. Extension of long term loans to Russia and Soviet Satellites.

6. Provide American aid to all nations regardless of Communist domination.

7. Grant recognition of Red China, and admission of Red China to the UN.

8. Set up East and West Germany as separate states in spite of Khrushchev's promise in 1955 to settle the Germany question by free elections under supervision of the UN.

9. Prolong the conferences to ban atomic tests because the US has agreed to suspend tests as long as negotiations are in progress.

10. Allow all Soviet Satellites individual representation in the UN.

11. Promote the UN as the only hope for mankind. If its charter is rewritten, demand that it be set up as a one-world government with its own independent armed forces. (Some Communist leaders believe the world can be taken over as easily by the UN as by Moscow. Sometimes these two centers compete with each other as they are now doing in the Congo.)

12. Resist any attempt to outlaw the Communist Party.

13. Do away with loyalty oaths.

14. Continue giving Russia access to the US Patent Office.

15. Capture one or both of the political parties in the US.

16. Use technical decisions of the courts to weaken basic American institutions, by claiming their activities violate civil rights.

17. Get control of the schools. Use them as transmission belts for Socialism, and current Communist propaganda. Soften the curriculum. Get control of teachers associations. Put the party line in text books.

18. Gain control of all student newspapers.

19. Use student riots to foment public protests against programs or organizations which are under Communist attack.

20. Infiltrate the press. Get control of book review assignments, editorial writing, policy-making positions.

21. Gain control of key positions in radio, TV and motion pictures.

22. Continue discrediting American culture by degrading all form of artistic expression. An American Communist cell was told to "eliminate all good sculpture from parks and

buildings," substitute shapeless, awkward, and meaningless forms.

23. Control art critics and directors of art museums. "Our plan is to promote ugliness, repulsive, meaningless art."

24. Eliminate all laws governing obscenity by calling them "censorship" and a violation of free speech and free press.

25. Break down cultural standards of morality by promoting pornography, and obscenity in books, magazines, motion pictures, radio, and TV.

26. Present homosexuality, degeneracy, and promiscuity as "normal, natural, and healthy."

27. Infiltrate the churches and replace revealed religion with "social" religion. Discredit the Bible and emphasize the need for intellectual maturity, which does not need a "religious crutch."

28. Eliminate prayer or any phase of religious expression in the schools on the grounds that it violates the principle of "separation of church and state."

29. Discredit the American Constitution by calling it inadequate, old-fashioned, out of step with modern needs, a hindrance to cooperation between nations on a worldwide basis.

30. Discredit the American founding fathers. Present them as selfish aristocrats who had no concern for the "common man."

31. Belittle all forms of American culture and discourage the teaching of American history on the ground that it was only a minor part of "the big picture": Give more emphasis to Russian history since the Communists took over.

32. Support any socialist movement to give centralized control over any part of the culture—education, social agencies, welfare programs, mental health clinics, etc.

33. Eliminate all laws or procedures which interfere with the operation of the Communist apparatus.

34. Eliminate the House Committee on Un-American Activities.

35. Discredit and eventually dismantle the FBI.

36. Infiltrate and gain control of more unions.

37. Infiltrate and gain control of big business.

38. Transfer some of the powers of arrest from the police to social agencies. Treat all behavioral problems as psychiatric disorders which no one but psychiatrists can understand or treat.

39. Dominate the psychiatric profession and use mental health laws as a means of gaining coercive control over those who oppose Communist goals.

40. Discredit the family as an institution. Encourage promiscuity and easy divorce.

41. Emphasize the need to raise children away from the negative influence of parents. Attribute prejudices, mental blocks, and retarding of children to suppressive influence of parents.

42. Create the impression that violence and insurrection are legitimate aspects of the American tradition; that students and special interest groups should rise up and make a "united force" to solve economic, political, or social problems.

43. Overthrow all colonial governments before native populations are ready for self-government.

44. Internationalize the Panama Canal.

45. Repeal the Connally Reservation so the US can not prevent the World Court from seizing jurisdiction over domestic problems. Give the World Court jurisdiction over domestic problems. Give the World Court jurisdiction over nations and individuals alike.

CHAPTER 7

Jesse Jackson *Is* Yasser Arafat

J esse Jackson *is* Yasser Arafat . . . without the guns, without the terror and without my grandmother's tablecloth on his head.

Let me explain.

Like many Americans, when September 11 happened, I had no clue as to what was happening in the Middle East. Honestly, the earth could have opened up and sucked the entire Middle East into its core, and it wouldn't have affected my life at all. Except maybe at the gas station.

Before September 11, my attitude toward the Middle East was, "Why don't you guys just get over it? Can't you just move on with your lives?" I had as little sympathy for them then as I do now for African-Americans who cry for reparations.

Get over it.

I will admit, on both topics, that that attitude is both shallow and lazy. But it is how I felt.

Do the people in the Middle East need to get over it? Yes, they do.

Do they need to come together and work something out? Yes, they do.

But what does the conflict between the Israelis and the Palestinians mean to us, here in America?

My wife and I took a trip there in 2002, and, yes—it changed our lives.

By the way, here's my pitch for Middle East tourism: Now's the time to go. There isn't anybody over there now. Who's insane enough to go on a tourist trip to the Middle East in the middle of all of this? I was. I went and actually felt secure, plus you can be in the Garden of Gethsemane alone for hours. That's right, no lines at the roller coasters at Six Flags over Bethlehem—now how much would you pay? But wait, there's more. . . .

I came back from my trip to Israel with a deeper understanding of what the Jews face and a profound respect and sadness for the plight of the Palestinians. But it also gave me a clearer vision of the African-American experience.

Before I went over, before September 11, I was like the typical American. A big, fat, lazy sloth who just wanted to sit on my couch eating HoHos and Doritos, just waiting for *Everybody Loves Raymond* on Monday night.

We didn't care about the Middle East—we didn't have to care. And why would we—unless we had some sort of Palestinian, Arab or Jewish background. We thought, "I wouldn't

give you two camels for the whole region quite frankly. I'm just tired of seeing it on my TV! Do whatever it is you have to do, divide up the land or don't, just let me get back to watching *American Idol.* Thank you."

When you start to look at it, it's easy to just pick a side and say, "Sharon is a killer and the Jews are stealing land" or "Arafat is a terrorist and the Palestinians want all the Jews dead." In reality, neither viewpoint holds the whole truth, and it takes time and effort to sort it out. Time that none of us are willing to spend on two incessantly warring peoples, located halfway around the world. (I mean, there are HoHos to eat.) Therein lies the problem most of us have. We have far too many fat, lazy, obese and apathetic tendencies to do anything but eat Marshmallow Fluff directly from the jar, and unless the Israelis or Palestinians can help us eat that Fluff from that jar more efficiently . . . screw them. The last thing we are going to do is educate ourselves about the political quagmire of the world's largest sand trap.

A Lack of Security

We get lost because the problem is too big. So, let's break it down. If we begin to look at the microcosm we can begin to see the macro. First, Americans need to understand the Israeli concept of security. The best example of this is: Get into your car— whatever city you live in—and drive fifteen minutes in any direction. When you get there, stop the car, put it in park and get out. Now, wherever you are, you are alone and in danger.

After driving a mere fifteen minutes, you are surrounded by people who want to kill you—just because of what you believe in and who you are.

Get it? Now get back in the car. Go another direction—not back toward home, but another direction. Drive thirty minutes. You're now in an entirely different place, surrounded by entirely different people.

And they want to kill you too.

Now get back in the car. Drive another twenty minutes. You're now in a third completely different place—this time you're in a different country. You may have noticed this when you passed the mine fields and razor wire.

And this time, the whole country wants to kill you.

Now drive forty-five minutes, and you're in another country, and the people there want to kill you as well.

Now get back in the car and drive six hours. You've now driven through three more countries where everyone wants to kill you. That's what it's like to live in Israel. That's what it means to be a Jew in the Middle East.

Imagine: You're living in a state smaller than the size of New Jersey, and everyone in Pennsylvania, New York and Delaware wants you dead, just because you are from the Garden State.

How did New Jersey get to be the Garden State? When I think of Jersey I think of oil refineries, gambling casinos, pollution, swamps and some guy named Tony

> flipping me off after he just ran over my puppy. Jersey
> really should be the "I Just Ran Over Your Puppy
> State."

Americans can't relate to a Middle East concept of security—
or the complete absence of it.

We don't understand what security means to Israelis, be-
cause, well, have you ever been to Texas? It's as far from
Brownsville to Texarkana, Texas, as it is from Texarkana,
Texas, to Chicago.

I worked at a radio station in Corpus Christi, which is the
second most humid place in existence, next to Hell when the
sprinkler system keeps going off because of the lake of fire
that continually burns but never is consumed. Anyway, I was
trying to drive out of Texas, and it was early morning when I
left Corpus Christi and late at night when I finally made it to
the border of Texas.

> ### *Understanding Israel*
>
> Lesson one:
>   You are surrounded by millions of people who hate
> you because of your race and they live literally right
> around the corner.

The next thing you have to consider to understand what the
Palestinians have gone through is that no one really cares

about them. Many say they do, or seem to, but their actions tell a different story. No one has ever cared. Not the Europeans who divided the country and not the other Arab nations, who have never really lifted a finger to help the Palestinians.

It's not about the plight of Palestinians or Jordan would have returned some of their land.

It's not about occupying territories or Syria would not be occupying Lebanon.

The Old Shell Game

Now, I feel real compassion for the Palestinians because I don't believe that people are that different. I don't believe that I am unique in my desire to do a hard day's work, go home, play with the kids, turn on the TV, kick back, have something good to eat and maybe occasionally *allow* my wife to experience the heat of my luxurious bed, if you know what I'm saying. (Fans of the radio show mentally insert martini music here.) That's not a Glenn trait, that's a human trait. The difference may be that they want a falafel and I want a cheese steak from Gino's in Philadelphia. But other than that, we're exactly alike.

All the Palestinians want is to go home, *have* a home, go play with the kids, have their family be safe and stop with all this nonsense. You think we're tired of seeing violence on the news? Imagine how tired the Palestinians are. Imagine how tired the Israelis are. Holy cow. They just want a solution. Sure, they want peace, but I think most in the region would settle for *calm*. I've said this for months, long before a new survey reported that 80 percent of the Palestinians think that Hamas is derailing their hopes for peace. While the average Palestinian is looking for a way to coexist, Hamas is publishing statements that "Every Jew needs to be killed and wiped off the face of the region."

The average Palestinian should not to be lumped in with the terrorists. To say that the Palestinians don't want peace, or that they are all terrorists is as offensive as saying that all Muslims want Americans dead or that all whites have a Robert Byrd hood in the trunk of their car.

No one in the Middle East has ever really helped the Palestinians stand on their own feet and become self-reliant. That's not the goal of Hamas, Arab dictators or Arafat. That would be too altruistic.

When we overthrew Saddam Hussein, do you know who were the first people the Iraqis kicked out of their houses? The Palestinians. Saddam Hussein had given a bunch of Palestinians houses that had belonged to Iraqis who were found disloyal to Saddam. Not because he cared about the Palestinians, but because they could be used to unite the Arab world against the Jews and Americans. The minute the strong arm was gone, those Iraqis kicked the Palestinians out of Baghdad: "Pack your things and find some other place to live." The same thing has happened to the Palestinians in place after place, time after time, country after country. Guess who had to sneak out of Jordan in the middle of the night dressed as a woman because the government was trying to arrest him? Yasser Arafat.

And part of "occupied" Palestine, if you will, is "occupied" by Jordan. But you don't see anyone up in arms telling Jordan to give the land back to the Palestinians, now do you? Of course not, because it's not politically expedient. It's not about them. It's about power, greed and misdirection.

The Palestinians, God bless them, are being used. They have always been used. Do they have a real case? Absolutely. Does Israel have a real case? Sure it does. Are there scumbags involved on both sides who just want mayhem, riots and death? You bet.

But the Palestinians are being used by their own leaders and by the leaders of the Arab world. The leaders of Egypt, Syria, Jordan and Saudi Arabia among others—allow their people to live in poverty, in filth, without any kind of real connection to the modern world in many ways. Has anyone ever wondered how these people keep control of their economically ravaged rat holes? They do it in two ways: by brute force and terror (i.e., Saddam Hussein) and by playing the classic shell game: "Don't look over here. Don't look over here. Look at that. Look at *that!* Your life sucks because of *those* people. They are the reason you suffer. Once they are stopped you can be free to prosper."

That's the oldest game in the book, and *that's* the same shell game that's being played with the Palestinians and here in America with the African-Americans.

When I was in Israel, I had one of those movie moments where the background became really sharp, really fast: I was walking in the streets of Jerusalem, which is cut up into several sections. I started off in the Palestinian area, and let me tell you—if you want fresh lamb eyeballs, I know the place to get them. Honestly, I didn't know animals *had* all those parts, let alone that they were edible. I'd want to blow myself up too, if that's what I was microwaving every day at the office for lunch—assuming I had a microwave or an office.

I was walking down these streets smelling things I didn't want to smell and seeing things that I'll never forget. It was dirty, dark and grimy, even the kids had filthy faces. You know how in a Disney movie, whenever there are orphans involved, there are always little English kids running around with soot on their faces saying, "Please, sir, if only I had a little bit o' chocolate, I could be like me other mates. Then I'd be happy. Please, sir." That's the way it looked. But this wasn't Disney. This was real.

As I walk down this street, the four-billionth business owner comes up to me—because remember, there are no tourists around and I'm a target on multiple levels—and he says, "I have great carpets for you, my friend. Come and look at my carpets and trinkets, my friend. . . ." And I turn around and look at him, trying to blow him off, and I say, "No thanks. I'm still trying to recover from the lamb eyeballs, but thanks for the carpet idea."

As I say this, I turn around and take a few steps away. Now I'm facing in a different direction, and there's a big stone archway. Through that archway, everything is clean. And when I walk through that gate, everything is bright. The shops are nice. Even the children seem clean.

That doorway was the threshold to my understanding of the Israelis and the Palestinians. In front of me, there were Israeli flags and clean streets. Behind me, there were plates of lamb eyeballs and dirty, grimy streets.

It's really no different from seeing downtown Detroit or Gary, Indiana. You know what those places in America look like, where you're afraid to get out of the car. But in America, you have to drive for twenty minutes or so before you get from the inner city to a suburb. Again, just like security, it's all about scale. In Israel, everything is so compact that there is no gradual transition. It's slums and nice, same space, different people.

In America, many believe that slums are slums because of economics. The houses are really old, everything's broken down and nothing works. But in Israel, on the other side of that archway, the houses and the buildings were just as old as in the Palestinian sections. It's more than pure economics. It comes from the attitude of the people: One side is being told, "You can't do it. You'll never make it." Their pride has either been taken away or maybe they drove it away themselves.

Messages of Slavery

Now let's break this down to Jesse Jackson and Yasser Arafat. I believe that they are in many ways, one and the same. Thus, if you understand the tactics of one, you will gain focus on the other. To understand Israel and the Middle East, you must understand Al Sharpton and Jesse Jackson. *They* are the ones who are standing in front of their followers saying things like, "You were enslaved by these people," and "These people did

you wrong and they owe you so much," or my personal fav—
"You'll never make it unless these people are forced to pay, because if they don't, they may do it again and you need the
cash." (Note: If it was Jesse, there would also be a lot more
rhyming.)

Just as with the attorneys who organize class-action law-
suits, it's not about the person who worked around asbestos.
It's about the attorney. Joe Asbestos gets a check for $5.65,
along with thousands of others, but the attorney gets millions.

They're throwing the shackles around their people, yet
again. They're chaining them up like slaves, yet again.

Who has a better case for a real ax to grind with the family
of man: the Jew or the African-American? You want to talk
about being offended by the Confederate flag? How do you
think Jews feel about the pyramids of Giza? "Gee, look over
here, Maxie. Here's a place where four of our distant relatives
were crushed into jelly beneath the stones by the Egyptians."
But you don't hear any Jews saying they should take down the
pyramids of Giza—why? Because it's not about slavery anymore for the Jews.

And besides, you don't hear a lot of Jews calling for the pyramids to be taken down, because Jews aren't really welcome
in Egypt. People are *still* trying to kill the Jews in Egypt.

But no, I don't think the Confederate flag should be flown.
That flag was flown again in the 1950s as a response to the civil
rights movement. It had nothing to do with celebrating the
history of the South before the Confederacy. It was a statement.

Do you have a right to fly it? Sure you do. Should you? I

don't think so. It means so much to so many people. The whole idea of states' rights—what a joke. What did the Civil War turn into? It turned into the issue of slavery. You don't fly the Nazi flag and say, "Well, World War II was about economic reform. That's all Nazism was. Oh, maybe he was wrong about the whole final solution thing but to me the Nazi flag stands for economic reform."

"Riiiiiight."

Look at the history of the Jews: The Jews were slaves, and when they weren't slaves anymore, people were chasing them down, trying to kill them—just because they were Jews. People are *still* trying to kill them.

But you can pretty much go anywhere in the United States—with the exception of a few places where they sell alligator meat on a stick—and you won't find anyone who's trying to kill African-Americans, with the exception of a couple of nut jobs. You have nut jobs in every race—just look at the Washington snipers.

White people were wrong to enslave Africans. Just as Africans are wrong for enslaving Africans today. It is a horrible, shameful thing. But what happened to African-Americans after slavery, until the 1960s, is just as important. Black America absolutely has a case to be made. But there's a lesson for the African-Americans and the Palestinians to be learned from the Jews.

The Jews were persecuted throughout history. They were enslaved, they were hated, they were hunted. There were signs in America that read, "No Blacks. No *Jews*. No Dogs."

It all boils down to three words: the Chosen People. One

group believes they are trying to escape slavery; the other has conquered it. The only thing separating the African-American from the Jew is the concept of the "Chosen People."

Jews are taught from an early age that they are different. They are taught that God Himself chose them to be a special people. Whether that's true or not is irrelevant. What matters is that they *believe* it.

What African-Americans are lacking is the belief that they too are God's chosen people. Now, other people in history have taken the idea of being chosen to an extreme, like Hitler deciding he was part of a superior race. But true strength comes from understanding who you really are and the power of the individual—not because of the color of your skin, not because of your religion, not because of background—but because you truly are an anointed one, you truly are God's chosen person and so am I. It's the belief that you can be great, no matter who's trying to stop you. That's the true power of believing you are chosen: not that you will be protected from harm, but that you can thrive in spite of it.

The Jews *conquered slavery*. African-Americans are told, "You are a victim."

African-Americans will be victims until the day they say, "I have conquered slavery. I am standing here because I am God's chosen person. I am part of God's Chosen People. No one can enslave me. I have everything I need to be complete and to succeed within me."

Now back to Israel and Palestine.

Yasser Arafat, Syria, Jordan, Egypt, Saudi Arabia—they don't care about the Palestinians and their plight.

Jesse Jackson and Al Sharpton don't care about the plight of the average black American either.

I make both those statements with the understanding that all of them would most likely disagree vehemently. I believe this to be true, because their messages are: "You need me. You need to stop those evil people. You need those people to get out of your way. You need this handout. Why am I not rhyming today?"

Those messages are messages of slavery.

A true empowerment message would be: "You don't need anyone but yourself. You are a strong person, you *can* make it." Or as my grandmother used to say: "If the world gives you lemons, make lemonade."

But that's not the message of anybody in the Middle East to the Palestinians. The Palestinians are being used by Arab leaders for their own political power. Why is it that Yasser Arafat has been in charge for so long and yet it wasn't until recently that the Palestinians had a constitution? Maybe because a constitution requires you to have a set of laws? If you set laws, the person in charge loses some power. Now, in theory, Arafat will have to live within those laws.

Who lives in the Middle East and claims to be for the Palestinians and wants to be bound by a set of laws? That would require reasonable people without any agenda of power and greed. That would require a leader.

Jesse Jackson might do some great things for the African-Americans, although nothing springs to mind, but for me, it's his motivation that comes into question.

I believe that Jesse Jackson is only doing the things he does because it enriches him and gives him more power.

I accuse the leaders of the Middle East of the same thing: The ongoing conflict between the Israelis and the Palestinians enriches them and gives them more power. More important, it allows them to play that shell game: "Yes, I know you're living in raw sewage, *but* have you seen what's going on in Israel?" It's a ruse, a red herring that they are using to retain their own power and keep the Palestinian people from looking at their own situation and demanding true leadership from their leaders.

Perhaps that's the critical key to understanding peace in the Middle East: Everyone's trying to make sure that their own people have *other* things to look at, because if they start looking at their own sand-hole situations, all those leaders are toast.

Is Islam Evil?

I have really struggled with Islam—boy, have I struggled with Islam—and my audience went with me on this journey from absolute Hell. There were no seventy virgins on this trip.

When I was looking for the answers on Islam, I went back and forth and took months of study, of prayer, of conversations, of seeking people out. I attended services at a mosque before I had a handle. There were times when I thought Islam was out-and-out evil and must be stopped, occasions when I thought it is the enemy of all mankind. There were other times when I thought, "Oh, Islam and its five pillars . . . what a great message of peace—let us now all hold hands and sing a song from Cat Stevens. Anything but 'Moonshadow.' " I would have these wild swings, depending on what I was reading, who I was talking to or what my latest experience was.

Only through time and reading and prayer did I come up with my answers on Islam and terrorists. Here they are:

- The terrorists are not only an enemy to the United States, they are an *absolute* enemy to all of Islam.
- Ninety percent of Islam is peaceful.
- Ten percent of Islam wants to see us dead.
- That 10 percent of the faith is composed of extreme radicals who have taken Islam through a time tunnel and twisted it into something ugly and barbaric.
- We *are* fighting a war against Islam. But only 10 percent of Islam.
- Muslims should be fighting this war right alongside us.

I'm not expecting Muslims to fight alongside us because they think that America is the greatest place in the world. Muslims should fight terrorism because it's going to destroy Islam for 90 percent of the rest of them.

I have news for you Muslims who happen to be reading this. If while watching TV you catch yourself thinking, "Oh, gee, well ninety percent of us are peaceful, but the terrorists do have a point, I just disagree with their methods!" Well, those extremist zealots have another group besides Jews and

Americans that they want converted or dead: *you.* That's right, they don't think you're Muslim *enough*—and you're next on their hit parade. Once they get rid of us, they're going to get rid of you, because you don't want to live *exactly* the way they say you should, exactly the way *they* interpret the Koran.

Islam hasn't had the equivalent of a Renaissance or the Enlightenment yet. They haven't had a Martin Luther yet. People who say that Islam is a barbaric and evil religion that wants death and destruction should go back in time and talk to the Christian Crusaders and say, "Ah . . . guys . . . are you sure Jesus wants you to be cutting babies in half?" What do you suppose would be their response to you?

My guess: The Crusaders' response would be very similar to the response of the barbarians we call terrorists.

Most likely, they would say that *you* had been sent by the Devil to corrupt the faith. They would call you an infidel and say you weren't Christian *enough,* and unless you were still sitting in your stylish, H. G. Wells time machine, you'd probably be receiving the sharp edge of their swords as well . . . all in the name of Christ.

All that fundamentalist Islam is lacking is about the last eight hundred years. I believe that one of the reasons they hate America so much is that they realize that the freedom of thought and religion in America will ultimately create the Islamic version of Martin Luther. And they're right. Their days are numbered.

The day that I decided to attend a mosque was the same day I told my producer Stu that I was coming to the conclusion that Islam *is* evil, that Islam *is* what we're fighting, that it's more than just 10 percent, that it was *all* of Islam. Stu went white. Mostly because he knows that if I really believed that, if I really felt it was important for my listeners to understand, I would have to talk about it on the air. And saying that in today's PC world could have ended my short and promising career.

But I said, "You know, I keep swinging back and forth. I want to see it in practice myself. I want to talk to an imam face-to-face. I want to look real Muslims in the eyes. I want to sit in a mosque and pray myself. I want to *feel* what Islam is."

So we went down to the killing fields of Philadelphia, the dirty streets without the lamb eyeballs. We walked into an old, abandoned school that had been transformed into a mosque and an Islamic school. And the first thing I heard when we walked in was, "Welcome, brother," the same way, with the same spirit that people are greeted in *my* church when they arrive and are called brother and sister. And it was said with sincerity. It was said even though I was wearing my little American flag lapel pin on my jacket. They had no idea why I was there or who I was, but they welcomed me in peace.

We took off our shoes and sat on the floor, along with everyone else, while they were going through their prayers, and we just listened and prayed for the truth. The imam told a story about how important it was to fast during Ramadan, what the benefits of fasting were and how when it's done in a prayerful way, it can strengthen the body and strengthen the soul.

Because, he said, "As in all religions, if fasting is not done in a prayerful way, it's just a diet." Good stuff, nothing hateful here, but it was just one visit.

On our way out, I picked up the magazine in the lobby, which was printed by the local people—this was important for me—this magazine was not printed for *me,* it was printed for the people of Islam who worship there.

And just like in any church bulletin at a time of war, there were stories in there about the ties to America, and how important American soldiers were. There were stories about how you can be a success in America and how important our freedoms are.

Those kinds of stories were either an elaborate system of lies or I was beginning to see the Real Islam.

Now, I try to always be guided by my feelings and by the spirit. I felt warmth in that mosque, and I felt peace. I felt friendship and understanding from those that we talked to. When I met with the imam afterward, we were both curious, frightened and skeptical of one another. I think we had that in common. But we sat down, and I just asked, "What's happening in the Middle East? What are your thoughts on people like Osama bin Laden? What are your thoughts on the Palestinians and the Israelis?"

While we disagreed on the some of the politics of the Middle East, we agreed on the principles: peace and freedom and an end to violence. That was the last day I had a swing on Islam. That's when I closed the book on understanding Islam. I finally understood that there are factions that want to tear this religion apart.

It's not the religion of my choice, but then again, many people don't choose mine either.

The War Isn't Over Yet

I talked to a senator from Kansas a while back, after the major battles in Iraq had ended, and he said, "We're now in the most dangerous place we've been in for a very long time. When the war was going on, everybody was worried, everybody was paying attention. Embedded reporters were disciplined if they gave any clue as to where our soldiers were. Now our soldiers are fully visible. Everyone knows where they are, and more important, America thinks the war is over."

This war is not over. We are only at the end of the beginning. All we've done is read the introduction to a book and closed it and said, "Good book! Wow, that was great!"

Well, I have news for you again: There are twelve more chapters after the introduction. We have dealt with the Middle East in one way for so long, we've lived by their understanding that "The enemy of my enemy is my friend."

We don't buy that anymore as a nation. We know now that the enemy of my enemy can *still* be my enemy. One of the most disturbing things that I read about in the newspapers these days is that we have a "covert war" going on in Iran—*we're funding terrorists* who want to topple the Iranian regime. *What?!* Have we not learned a thing? That's how it all started with Osama.

And, Saudi Arabia, I have news for you: You can play the "We're a happy little sand country" commercials all you want, but that doesn't make you our friend. That's public relations. Only your actions will make you our friend.

But the leaders of Saudi Arabia can't afford to be our friends. They can't afford to root out terrorism, because to do that means to take on the religious extremists, and it's those religious extremists who actually *give* them their power.

The most important thing to understand about terrorism—and God forbid that something on the scale of 9/11 happens again (or that it's happened in the time it takes for this book to come out)—the most important thing to understand about terrorism is that we no longer live in a world where we can sit back on our couch for long periods of time and eat ice cream from the carton. We have to remain vigilant; we have to remain focused on what really is happening.

It Was Never About Weapons of Mass Destruction

If you go back to one of the first, post–September 11 speeches George Bush gave and you look at all of his subsequent speeches, you'll find that he's spelling something out plainly, even though he's not saying it overtly. Saying this overtly would be political suicide in the rest of the world. You think Bush is unpopular in France now? Imagine what they'd think if he spoke clearly about what we're doing.

We're changing the face of the Middle East.

We're remaking the Middle East, and you *are* either for us or against us, because we are *not* living with terrorism any longer.

The terrorists are fighting for their lives right now and we haven't rooted them out yet. They've still got a lot of fight left in them.

But we have more.

We're changing the face of the Middle East, just as we changed the face of Germany.

We're changing the face of the Middle East, just as we changed the face of Japan.

Japan is a country that was radically different before World War II, very disciplined and rigid with their laws imposed upon the citizens by an emperor appointed to that role by God.

Gee, sounds almost like a fundamentalist, Islamic country.

And when we won World War II, the people said the same things they are currently saying about the Middle East, "You'll never be able to change *those* people. They can't begin to understand freedom and democracy."

But again, people aren't any different from you and me. They want to control their own lives and destiny. What we did in the 1940s is we went over and planted the seeds of democracy by leaving a constitution. Even if their government doesn't exactly mirror ours, the people are free and the laws are made by the people, not forced on them.

A clear example of this is Israel: Take five minutes some day and look into the way a newly elected prime minister cob-

bles together power in the Knesset—their version of Congress. It's enough to make you run to Home Depot for a case of duct tape. You think our system of government is insane, you should see *their* system! But you know what? The Israelis are free, they've designed their own democracy and they are flourishing.

The same goes for Japan and Germany: We may disagree on structure, politics and policy, but each of these systems reflects the same principles—life, liberty and the pursuit of happiness. The United States didn't go over and build a U.S. Capitol in Tokyo or Berlin. We ensured a secure and stable environment and then gave them the tools of freedom to work with and said, "This is how you start. Here's your constitution. Now you take it from here." And you know what they did? They did the American thing: They took something good and made it something great. For a while, in the 1970s and 1980s they were even kicking our butts. And I don't know about you, but unless you were working for Lee Iacocca in Detroit, none of us really wanted to take Japan apart.

Hey, they were doing a great thing. They were doing what *we* should have done: constantly expand our horizons. Instead, we had become morally and physically undisciplined and complacent.

For those who are crying that America is building an empire, I ask you to point to the U.S. occupying forces in the former Axis power countries. You can't, because they don't exist. We don't occupy—we ask for just enough ground to bury our dead.

We are helping others fully experience the blessings that come from realizing the inalienable rights that each of us are endowed with by our creator.

A message to the naysayers: If you want to know what America is doing and what the future holds, read history. What the Allies accomplished against people embittered by fascism last century is about to happen again. I find it ironic that the tables have been turned on America. In World War II we were the ones coming last for dinner. As all of Europe begged us to take a seat, we said, "It's not our fight and who are we to tell Germans who to elect and how to run their country?" Many even claimed the Germans had a right to be angry and that Europe had brought this on themselves because of the Versailles Treaty. Once again, I remind you if you want to know the future, learn the past.

Now we are the ones begging France and the rest of the world to open their eyes and see the gathering storm on the horizon. Come take your seat at the table of man. As Alanis Morissette might say, "It's like a black fly in your Chardonnay" to hear them almost parrot back our words from over sixty years ago, "This isn't our war. They are not bothering us."

Well, now they *are* bothering us and that's the ultimate challenge in America, isn't it? That's what everything in America boils down to: I don't have a problem with what you do, as long as you don't bother me. Once you start bothering me, then we have a problem. (Sometimes it's too late.)

So when people from the Middle East started screwing with us, that's when we started having a problem with them:

"You want to blow yourselves up? Fine. You want to strap explosives to yourself? Allah be praised. You want to drive into a crowded falafel house or hummus hut and blow up your own people? Good for you! We're going to go to the movies Friday night. Thanks for stopping by."

> In Germany they came first for the Communists and I didn't speak up because I wasn't a Communist. Then they came for the Jews and I didn't speak up because I wasn't a Jew. Then they came for the trade unionists and I didn't speak up because I wasn't a trade unionist. Then they came for the Catholics and I didn't speak up because I was a Protestant. Then they came for me—and by that time no one was left to speak up.
>
> —Martin Niemöller 1892–1984

Then came September 11. Now we're awake, now we care. And we're not going to play the games you've been playing. We can no longer afford to.

Hey, camel countries, do you know *why* you guys are having rock sandwiches and washing them down with glasses of sand for lunch? Because there's no security in your region. You are so busy terrorizing each other that you couldn't even build a Fiat . . . and Fiats suck.

Nobody wants to invest or do business in your region because you're going to blow each other up and take down my brand new McDonald's franchise with you!

Once there's security, *then* you can start to have commerce. Once you have real lasting commerce, then you'll see: Your lives will change.

The only way you can really have lasting commerce is to be secure and free. And the first step to those is a constitution.

So we'll leave you one. Catch you later.

Back to peace in Israel: The first thing that has to be done is stomp out terrorism. Hezbollah, Islamic Jihad, Al Qaeda, Al-Aqsa Brigades and Hamas: All that has to be burned out with a scorched-earth policy. There also must be zero tolerance for that kind of thinking on the Israeli side: Anyone who justifies terror through death and destruction so he can build the new temple or stop the "occupation" must be viewed and treated as a pariah.

We've got to stop terrorism first. People think terrorism is a symptom and the cause is poverty. I think it is just the opposite: Terrorism isn't caused by poverty; poverty is caused by terrorism. Terror is a tool used by those seeking power to keep the masses in need of their answer. Once we wipe that out, once we plant the seeds of democracy and water them with security and commerce in surrounding countries, people will begin to understand the concept that they can do it themselves, they can make it on their own, they can change their own lives for the good. Once those things start to take root in people, then you'll experience seeing Arabs having the prosperity that Israel has.

What ultimately hacks off the Arab world is that Israel is prosperous. They've taken a dusty, dirty desert of a place and turned it green. How is that possible? Here's an idea, guys: *You can do it too.* Once you have pockets of Arab nations succeeding, stable and a healthy economy with food on their tables—done by Arabs—then Hamas and Al Qaeda's worst nightmare happens: *Democracy will spread like wildfire.*

People in other Arab countries will *want* democracy.

If we don't snuff out the terrorists, there will never be any kind of legitimate economy in the Middle East. People will always be starving and looking to blame it on somebody—anybody.

Another danger will come from the extremists during the initial growth of democracy. They're going to point their fingers at the pockets of prosperity and say, "Well, they're only prospering because they're in league with the Zionists; they're in league with the devil, and you are not gaining ground because you are not Islamic *enough*."

But as all the pieces fall into place, we will change the face of the "Axis of Evil" the same way we changed the face of Europe in World War II.

Humiliation and the Past

The last critical piece in really understanding the Middle East is the importance that humiliation plays in Arab society. It's an easy generalization but a useful starting point. We witnessed an example of that after the Iraq war. What were the Palestinians and those in Egypt and Syria saying? They were upset because Saddam didn't fight "to the finish," which was to them another example of "Arab humiliation." They didn't look at the torture chambers that were there and the fact that the Iraqi people had been freed. They saw only the Arab nation humiliated once again.

They didn't have to give the United States credit for doing anything good. They didn't have to say, "Hey, those Americans did a great job." They could have just ignored that or said, "Well, the Americans did horrible things, but we're going to help the Iraqi people. Look at what they've gone through. Oh my gosh." But they didn't say that. They were just upset that Saddam Hussein had lost without putting up a good fight. Anwar Sadat's daughter was quoted saying that she hopes "the Americans fail in Iraq *even if it makes it worse for the Iraqi people* because of the humiliating defeat brought onto the Arab people by the American troops." My italics, her words.

Here in America, we don't dwell on our past battles. We don't beat our breasts and cry, "I hate those Vietnamese for what they did to us in 1968. I hate them. I hate them. I *hate* them!" And that's only thirty-five years ago. Arabs resent things that happened one thousand years ago.

"Get over it" is a phrase that comes to mind.

You know whose fault that whole Vietnamese thing was? Ours. Not theirs. *Ours.* We were the ones who made the mistakes. We were the ones who got into the wrong battle. We were the ones who fought it incorrectly.

But that's not the case over in the Arab world. It's always "them" humiliating the Arabs, whoever "they" or "them" are. This time it's us.

So many people scratch their head in America and say,

Here I am directing the first live commercial radio drama in over 40 years, as heard on XM Radio.

Listening to final production mix downs.

After doing a total of maybe 40 hours of talk radio, I was asked to host a national show. Here, Stu and I are at Rush Limbaugh's EIB studio in New York.

Chatting with former president George Bush in his home in Kennebunkport.

At 15, at KBRC radio in Mount Vernon,
Washington.

"Jingoistic" from birth,
I am 9 here, waving the flag.

My family's life changed the day we were baptized as members of our church.

Mom and Dad at the bakery.

Here, my best friend and on-air partner Pat Gray is seen explaining to a very sad me that being a banana is just part of being a bottomed-out Top 40 morning guy.

With Matt Drudge: No matter what the mainstream media may tell you, they hammer this guy because he tells the truth, and you can count on one hand the number of times he's been wrong.

That's me in my state-of-the-art network studios in Philadelphia.

Try to tell me you were more friendless as a kid than I was.

With Tania and producer Jeff Fisher on our trip to Israel.

An insider's view of Stu and me discussing the show during a break.
Notice that Stu is watching TV as he only hears me saying, "Blah, blah, blah."

After a long weekend attending rallies, I make my way back to the airport, accompanied by audio and video wizard Eric Chase.

"What the heck? I can't begin to understand their thinking."
Of course not. You couldn't unless you understand this fundamental difference: They're tied to the past. We're running to the future.

When you understand that Arab culture looks to past glories and past humiliations and that everything is rooted in yesterday's transgressions, you can understand why we see things so radically different.

Americans always see a better tomorrow. That's what we loved about Ronald Reagan. He saw that shining city on the hill. He reminded us that it was still morning in America. We are still reaching for it and striving for it, and it is ever elusive.

The Arab world sees the past. They always want to right the wrongs of the past.

Most Americans are too lazy, too slovenly and didn't do well enough in history to even *understand* our past. So we *have* to go forward.

And we will.

There Is Always Hope

Right before the first anniversary of September 11, I had the opportunity to sit down and talk to George Bush 41, father of George Bush 43. It was my wife's thirtieth birthday, and we went up to Kennebunkport and spent some time with the Bushes in their home. Before the interview began, before we were rolling tape, I told him what a special day it was for me to be able to meet him, but not for the reasons he might think.

When my oldest daughter, Mary, was born, she had several strokes at birth and was diagnosed with cerebral palsy. I'll never forget when the doctor was standing there in the intensive care room, while my daughter was still all wired up to all kinds of monitors.

They had just taken a CAT scan, and there she was, this little, teeny newborn, her whole body fit in the headrest of the CAT scan. The doctor said, "I want to show you some film. Just so you know, black on the film is blood. Black is bad. This should look very opaque."

He took the films out of the big manila envelope, and we all stood there looking up at the fluorescent lights on the ceiling.

My daughter's brain was almost all black.

I said, "What does this mean?"

And the doctor said, "It's hit almost every center: It's hit her incoming speech, her outgoing speech. It's hit her motor control."

He said, "If this happened to you, you'd never walk again, you'd never talk, you'd never be able to feed yourself again."

I said, "Well, it didn't happen to me. It happened to my daughter. *What does this mean?*"

He said, "I want you to know that she may never function at any real level. But there is always hope."

A few days later, I brought my daughter home. I was standing in the living room with the television on. It was during the 1988 election campaign. George and Barbara Bush were on television, I was standing in the living room, holding my infant daughter in my arms, with the wires coming off of her, a machine next to me monitoring her breathing, and I looked

up at the television as they were asked about abortion. Their answer was that every child's life is worth living.

George Bush looked right at me through my television and said, "We had a daughter, Robin, who contracted a deadly disease and the doctors told us she wasn't going to live very long, that she was only going to live a few weeks. Well, it turned out she lived for a year and a half. And we learned more from her in that year and a half than we had from anyone else. It was the most important time of our lives." They were both weeping at the time.

And then he said, "The doctors can be wrong. The doctors don't always know what they're talking about. *The doctors can be wrong.*"

It was as if he were speaking directly to me, in my home in Phoenix, Arizona, with my daughter in my arms. He was talking right to me and telling me, "There's hope. There's *always* hope."

So I told this story to the president, and I said, "I want you to know that this day is such a special day for me—not just because I'm meeting a former president, but because today, coincidentally, is the day my daughter first walks through the doors of her high school. You were right: The doctors were wrong."

When people say there will never be peace in the Middle East, hold out for hope, because you'll never know what surprising and miraculous things are right around the corner.

There is always hope.

Tolerance

Throughout this book, we have talked about political correctness. Political correctness is a poison, a poison that has deviously infiltrated our society in some parts and been welcomed with open arms in others. It has taken the strongest and darkest feelings that we possess, and driven them deep into our souls. It has created a generation of liars.

I am one of those liars.

For years I have been hiding something that has not only eaten away at the very fabric of my being, but has also been fuel for unending internal embarrassment and guilt. I have kept this secret for almost my entire life.

I guess I hoped these feelings would just go away. I thought that one day, I would just wake up and realize that it was just a stupid fling. It was just innocent experimentation. However, with each passing day, my feelings grew stronger.

Still, I tried to repress. Why? I tried to repress because of political correctness. I thought that if I admitted the love I had been hiding, society would reject me. They would make me a pariah. I could lose my job, my material possessions, even my family.

Sometimes though, you have to stand up and say the unpopular thing. Today, I have to stand up and *be* the unpopular thing.

It all started one day when I was twelve. I was living in a suburb of Seattle, Washington. I was a relatively normal twelve-year-old, complete with an uncomfortable social presence and newly raging hormones. That's when I found my true love. I had been close with this person for a while, but nothing had ever happened romantically. Sure, I had looked this person's way a few times and got that nervous feeling in my stomach—but I had been taught that this love was forbidden.

Then came the fair. We went together for every year that I can remember. We walked around, ate fried dough, looked at the animals, played the games and rode the rides. There was one ride, however, that would change my life: the Ferris wheel.

We waited as the line snaked through the metal dividers. We boarded and began our trip up to what felt that day like the top of the world. Right away, I could tell that this was not your everyday Ferris-wheel ride. We kept glancing at each other and then quickly looking away, both of us understanding what we felt, but neither one giving in for fear of social stigma. My hand brushed this person's . . . my palms began to sweat . . . my hands began to shake. Just then, the Ferris wheel came to a complete stop. We didn't know what was wrong, and we didn't care. Here we were, stopped at the summit of this giant wheel . . . alone.

I looked deeply into this person's eyes, and reached out to softly touch this person's face. I leaned in and I kissed this person.

I kissed my sister.

First our lips met, seconds later our tongues. I ran my fingers through her silky hair and felt her soft skin. It was the height of passion and the moment I knew who my true love was. Suddenly the wheel creaked back into motion, and we both leaned back to our own sides of the cart, smirking. We knew we had done something so wrong, but at the same time, something so very right.

Since then we have met in secret several times, and while those meetings have also been magical, I feel we will never recapture the enchantment of that evening on the Ferris wheel, until we can tell the world about our love. So that is what I am doing here today.

Sometime before this book is released, I will tell my wife about this. I don't want her to find out the way that you just did. I will tell her, and she will either accept me for who I am, or do what many of you are doing right now, saying to yourself how "disgusting" or "deviant" or "perverted" *my* choices are.

Maybe what you should be saying to yourself is, "Why do I feel the need to comment on other individuals' wants, needs and rights?"

My sister and I are in love. Our love does not affect you. Your opinion does not affect me. As Americans, we are given the right to pursue happiness. This is all that we—as a couple—are asking. Making judgments and pointing fingers demonstrates a thoughtless hatred proving that you have lived in a sheltered world without diversity of thought and culture. I realize that I am different . . . but am I so different that I haven't earned the right to love?

Look, I'm not forcing my opinions on you. I don't ask you to live the way that I live. I simply ask you to be *tolerant*.

Ask yourself this question. Does what I do with my sister in the privacy of my own home affect your life in any way? The answer is absolutely not. My relationship with my sister won't hurt your marriage, it won't dismantle your family, it won't make you love your sister the way I do. It will simply make two people happy. It will make two people complete. Please accept us for who we are.

How can anyone ask another human being to reject his natural instincts in an effort to conform to society's version of what is appropriate? The bottom line is, I will make my own decisions. Entering into a relationship with my sister isn't wrong—it is a choice, and how dare you attempt to disallow my freedom of choice.

While our love is true and everlasting, there will still be some who question. Fear is a normal human response when presented with change and human development. Are there legitimate concerns? Sure.

Many ask, "Do you want children?" The answer is yes. We are completely immersed in our devotion for each other. We will make love. However, love is not selfish. We *will not* risk the unfortunate side effects that our expressions can produce. We *will not* risk the health of a child being born with serious birth defects. We *will not* burden society with a child of special needs. In my heart, I know that if we had met in the "traditional" way, we would have been married and enjoying a large family by now. But nontraditional questions have nontraditional answers. Therefore, we will both be sterilized. The risk of adverse health consequences to the child will be gone. Our desire to care and love another human being will not be.

This is why my sister and I have decided to adopt. Unlike many "normal" couples, our relationship is not based on sex. It is based on a committed loving relationship that could nurture a young soul like no other. Our special bond and the persecution we must endure will only make us more compassionate and understanding parents. We will adopt a child that is poor and underprivileged. A child that society has forgotten. A child that you may believe is "disposable."

Still there will be those closed-minded people who will attempt to destroy our home. There will be some who would rather a child be parentless, living their lives going from one dangerous foster home to another. Still clinging to the crutch of intolerance. This amazes me. Even with a child's life at stake, judgmental hatred still rules. Do you live in "the Real America"? I know I do. I live in an America where society will not risk the life of a child just to damn me for what I do in my own bedroom. I live in an America where they are tolerant of other views, religions and sexual orientations. I live in a place where people love their brothers and accept them for the

people they are. In my America, you can be free to choose your own path in life, as long as it doesn't hurt someone else.

At the very least, I beg you to show my family respect. Please do not refer to us as an "incestuous" couple. Keep the hate language to yourself. We prefer to think of the gift we have been given as "familial love."

Have you accepted me yet? If no, why not? I have done all the steps. First I made a grand declaration showing my courage. Then I used words like "hatred," "judgment" and "persecute," therefore connecting anyone who doesn't agree with me to these negative words. After that, I pulled on your heartstrings and pleaded with sad puppy dog eyes, using more specifically selected language such as "accept me" and "diversity of thought" and of course "choice." I then simultaneously reasoned with your kindness and laziness creating an option of inaction fueled by empathy. And finally, those who control the language control the argument. That's why I changed the word "incestuous" into "familial love" creating a new group of bigots, who will still call it incest.

This is how it's done. By now, you probably have realized that I am not in love with my sister. I mean, she's great and everything, but I don't want to marry her, make out with her or have kids with her. I wrote this to make a point.

I told a similar story on the air one day and stuck to it for a full hour. At the beginning there were nonstop calls looking for my head. Telling me I was perverted, disgusting and wrong to love my sister. About thirty minutes into it, I started getting calls saying "Hey, it's not my choice, man, but if this is what makes you guys happy, then it's okay by me." Imagine that. Being turned around on something as big as incest in a half hour (or a few pages)! Don't allow the manipulation of language to fool us or to mask the principles that are at stake. "Freedom fighters" are terrorists, "Adult-child sex" is pedophilia, "Pro-Choice" means "pro-abortion" and "Low-Fat" means "tastes like cardboard." Whenever you see new words, understand the old axiom: Change the language and control the agenda.

Glenn Beck Fun Fact

When I did this hour on the air, we had just started in syndication. I sold the "I love my sister" thing for the whole hour, ready to reveal the truth at the top of the next hour. Unfortunately, George W. Bush decided to make a speech, and many of our stations decided to preempt the conclusion of the incest story for Bush. So while I was saying, "Okay, I don't want to marry my sister," they were hearing him talk about taxes. I can't help but think, there is still some old lady somewhere who won't listen to my show anymore because "that pervert made out with his sister."

So, what's the point? Why did I spend a whole chapter talking about a committed loving relationship with my sister? I did it because right now there is an organized ongoing effort to try to bend your values. To slowly shape your deepest beliefs into toleration and eventually acceptance.

Now, sometimes we really do need to make changes. Sometimes, our long-held beliefs are dead wrong. I'm not trying to say, "Well, we used to believe in slavery, so now we should go back to it!" I'm trying to say, "Look at the individual issue. Connect with your heart, your mind and your God. Honestly question the source, and honestly question yourself. Just remember, the truth never changes . . . it's just our understanding of the truth that does."

CHAPTER 9

Business: The Engine of America

Growing up in a small town in Mount Vernon, Washington, was not a pleasant experience for a boy who wanted to live in New York.

Ever since I was eight or nine years old, I wanted to work in Rockefeller Plaza. I don't know why—I don't know how an eight-year-old even knows about Rockefeller Plaza when you live ninety miles north of Seattle. But *I* did. I wanted to work at NBC. I knew exactly what I wanted to do: I wanted to be on the radio.

Mount Vernon, Washington, couldn't have been farther away from where I wanted to be. It's a little community in Skagit Valley that, by the way, is the largest tulip producer outside of Holland. Whoopee!

My dad was a baker, as was his dad before him. My dad also knew what he wanted to do when he was eight years old. He wanted to decorate and bake cakes, and he wanted to make beautiful pastries.

My dad and I weren't very close to each other when I was growing up, because he was working all the time. But his work wasn't like other dads' work, I guess, because my father loved his work. He loved it so much you could see it, and I would watch my dad make cakes and pastries and bread.

Watching my dad ice the cakes was like watching an artist, because he could make a glob of shapeless icing come out of the bottom of a tube and magically turn it into a rose. This was before everything became the little sugar press-ons that they put on cakes today. What my dad did took him *time*. What my dad did was art.

The real reason I thought he was an artist was the expression on his face. My dad absolutely loved his work, and when people came into his shop and told him they appreciated his work, he would just beam.

I must have been about eight years old when a TV commercial came out for Home Pride Buttertop Bread. They said on the commercial, "We split the top and pour butter in, so the butter bakes right in."

I went to my dad, and said, "Dad! We should do that!"

My father was crushed. He looked at me and said, "Glenn, that's called advertising. We *do* do that. *Everybody* does that."

I wish I had learned more about cooking and baking from him back then, but I just wasn't interested. I remember he always told us that lots of people could make something *taste* good, but the real secret was to make something look as good as it tasted and taste as good as it looked. That's where the art comes in. His food looked good and tasted wonderful because of what it meant to him. It wasn't just a cookie or just a loaf of bread. It was an extension of him.

I met a guy recently in Tulsa, Oklahoma, whose name is Don Conner. He owns a little seafood restaurant called Da Boat. When I went into Don's restaurant in a little Oklahoma strip mall down the street from Oral Roberts University, I not only enjoyed his food, I also enjoyed watching Don work. Here he is, this chef, wearing these big red, white and blue chef pants . . . .

I don't know what it is about chef pants—where do you get those and who was the first guy who said, "I need pants *uglier* than golf pants—and *then* I can cook"?

But there was Don, wearing these ugly pants, walking around, cooking and greeting people in his restaurant. In came this older woman with a boy who I think was her grandson and they sat at the table next to us. The grandson was probably twelve, maybe fourteen.

As I eavesdropped on their conversation, I heard that it was his birthday. So here's this fourteen-year-old kid out on his birthday—with *Grandma*. This kid really didn't have the best attitude. He was not having what you would call a "blast" with Grandma.

But he sat there at the table politely as they ate and made conversation. At the end of the meal, Don came over and said, "I understand it's your birthday." The boy looked up, kind of hesitantly and said, "Yes. Yes it is." Don said, "We've got to get you some cake or something. What do you want for your birthday?" And the kid said, "No, really, I don't want any dessert."

The real reason the kid didn't want any dessert was that he just wanted to go home to his Sony PlayStation. *"Please,"* he was thinking, "let this nightmare with Grandma end. Let me leave or kill me now. *Please!"*

That's when Don actually sat down at the table and said, "Come on, you've got to have *something."* He wasn't trying to "up-sell" or make a buck. He was seriously interested in this kid and really wanted him to have something to celebrate his birthday. He ended up bringing the kid one of his bread puddings with a candle in it—and the boy and Grandma were both glad he did.

More than the food, more than the bread pudding, I enjoyed watching Don. He reminded me of my dad. They both enjoyed just working their craft.

I often think the American dream has very little to do with money.

The American dream is really about making life better for our kids. Money can grease the skids, of course, and money can make things a little easier for all of us down the road. But when we say we want a better place for our kids, when we say we want a better America, that doesn't mean we just want them to have bigger houses.

I know people who have huge houses, with tremendous square footage, yet they have little room for real pleasure in their lives.

In business, the American dream revolves around doing the right thing, making a decent buck, but more important, digging your job. I am the most blessed person on planet Earth. I get up every morning and I'm excited to go to work.

That's the way my dad was, that's the way Don seems to be: excited to go to work.

That's the American dream. Most of us don't have it though. Most of us slugs have to get up in the morning and go to a job we hate, where we're making something of no value.

You couldn't pay me enough money to live that way. Okay, you probably could, but that's for another chapter.

For me, it's all about making things of value, and the only way things have value is when the work comes from your heart. That's where all of my dad's recipes came from. My grandmother told me once, "You can't get the recipe right unless you add the right amount of love." I think it is bigger than she meant it: It's not just the love she had for me, it's the love of whatever it is you're doing. Maybe it's just bigger than I understand it.

A Picnic Table for My Mom

Mount Vernon was a small town that was just great—the perfect little town, like so many perfect little towns in America—until the mall moved in.

Once the mall moved in, everything changed, because everybody wanted to do their shopping at the new mall. This was back in 1972 or 1973, when malls started to crop up all over America and the main streets started to decay and the towns started to die. In Mount Vernon, before the mall moved in, downtown was the place where I would stand on the street corner, or be on my father's shoulders, and watch Santa come down the street in a fire truck. And there was only one Santa, and he was at the Sears store.

When our little town started to decay, people started to move out and businesses started to be boarded up.

My mom knew the town was dying. So did my dad. They wanted to save our family business, so they appealed to all the other business owners, and they said, "Guys, this mall is going to kill us and our way of life is going to be over. We have to act now."

It was 1974, just before the Bicentennial, so my folks decided that they would push "Mount Vernon, *Washington*." They thought that would be a unique angle on the West Coast, where "old" means 1920. They thought, "Maybe we can make this a colonial village, like Williamsburg or Mount Vernon, Virginia." Basically what it meant was that they wanted to throw some brick on the front of the buildings and make it something a little different. Maybe something "quaint." Oh no, there's that word that always seems to get me into trouble.

Not many in the town really liked the idea, and we, I always felt, became outcasts, mainly because we were the family that was always dressed up in colonial clothes. For parades around the area my dad and I would dress in the Revolutionary War uniforms my mom made us, and my eldest sister, Coletta, would play Betsy Ross. Except her giant hoopskirt was actually a VW Beetle underneath. Oh, she loved it. Really.

We were a weird family.

A few stores added the brick, put gaslight in front, but it was spotty. It fought with itself. The old businesses just boarded up when the owners got sick or died, others gave up and decided to make the move to go into the mall. And a few places, like my parents' bakeshop, decided not to abandon the town and held on for a time.

By the time we moved out of the town, because my parents got a divorce, it was a town torn apart with a growing number of empty buildings.

Their colonial movement had failed.

I went back a few years ago, and to my surprise, they've made Mount Vernon, Washington, into the "quaint" town my folks dreamed about. The town is thriving again. The shops are full. The big Sears building doesn't have a Sears anymore, but the windows aren't all soaped up either. They changed the architecture of some of the buildings and they added some brick alleyways and brick streets.

The brick my parents dreamed about.

I was walking down one side street, and I came across a picnic table, and there on the table was a plaque that read IN MEMORY OF MARY BECK.

Thirty years later, twenty-five years after my parents' divorce, twenty-three years after my mom's suicide, IN MEMORY OF MARY BECK.

When I saw that picnic table, everything changed. It showed me that downtown rebirth is possible, but it can't happen overnight. Just as my mom and dad had dreamed, the town came back to life.

Downtowns are important, because they represent small business. They represent the engine of America. And that engine, I got news for you, is not Nordstrom's—great store, I shop there myself—and that engine is not Sbarro (although I enjoy a good mall pizza just as much as the next guy).

The engine of America is the small store where Mom and Pop have a dream and struggle to make ends meet.

That's what downtowns are in the Real America: individual dream factories, where somebody says, "I will open a bakery and I'll be the best baker ever."

Or it's Da Boat: "I'm going to have a seafood restaurant—in Tulsa, of all places—and it's going to be great and people are going to come, because *I love making the food.*"

Not because the Sbarro people tell me that I have to add so-many meatballs and x-number of pepperoni to every pizza. That's not what it's about. That's what *malls* are all about.

Downtowns are about something real, something of intrinsic value, something authentic.

Bill's Khakis

There's a company I do business with called Bill's Khakis, a longtime sponsor on our show. Bill Thomas is one of the coolest men I've ever met. I call Bill "Bing," because he is Bing Crosby, without the orange juice, the golf clubs and the weird family life. But he has that kind of 1940s sensibility to him. In fact, when I went to a Christmas party for Bill's Khakis, a Christmas party for all of his employees, Bill was wearing his father's old plaid blazer from the 1950s.

Bill's dad was involved in his town of Reading, Pennsylvania, and I think that Bill's dad and my dad had a lot in common. They both believed in the importance of the little community in which they lived.

Years ago, Bill heard from a few friends that you could get some great khakis that were authentic World War II issue at an army surplus store down the road from his college. So he cranked up his jeep and drove to the source of the rumor. There he found the real McCoy: big, roomy, deep-pocketed, plain-front khakis that were built to last a hundred years.

After wearing them for a few months, Bill went back to the store for a more. But they were gone. The owner of the store said that the surplus had dried up but he still had some gas masks and live grenades.

After a thorough search for a new pair that matched the quality of his World War II favorites, Bill came to the conclusion that no one was making great khakis today. It didn't seem right that we could put a man on the moon but not make a pair of khakis as well as we did fifty years ago.

With little to go on but a $5,000 bank loan cosigned by his mother, he found a small-town factory near his home willing to replicate a small production run of his originals and started selling khakis out of the trunk of his car.

It took four years and ten part-time jobs to get the business to the point where it could support a full-time effort. One by one, consumers and retailers got into Bill's Khakis.

What Is Bill's Khakis?

As fascinated as we are with the future, our hearts lie in the past. Old movies, books, vintage photographs; these are the places we go to connect. Having a father who passed on when he was young heightened Bill's need to stay in touch with his Dad's world and the ideals it represented. Finding a vehicle to do so was something Bill never thought possible.

He found it in a purely American product: that pair of original World War II army-issue khakis that he stumbled upon while in college.

By 1989, after having read one too many books by Ayn Rand, the idea of creating Bill's Khakis had taken on such strong philosophical importance to him, that he had to quit a job he loved and move home to Reading, Pennsylvania, to get on with his ideals. Not only did these khakis represent a forgotten piece of Americana, but they were the manifestation of everything Bill felt was virtuous about business, entrepreneurship and just about everything else. This was his chance to start the quintessential American company.

It made perfect sense. All Bill had to do was resurrect all the superior qualities found in his original pair of vintage khakis. Then, once the product was perfected, never change a thing.

Bill still refuses to make anything outside of the United States. It costs Dockers under ten bucks to make a pair of pants; God knows where they make them. For Bill to make a pair of khakis here in the United States costs him about forty bucks.

He could make a lot more money. He could have a lot more profit. He could sell a lot more pants because they'd be cheaper, but Bill believes in America. He believes in that small town. And he doesn't want to make Bill's Khakis outside of the United States.

Today, more than twelve years since the first pair, Bill's Khakis employs twenty people, not including a small factory down the road that Bill's has saved from going out of business, and is working on the second factory now.

The pants are about $100 or so a pair, but when you wear them, you're wearing more then just a pair of pants—you're wearing an idea.

You're wearing somebody's dream.

You're wearing downtown.

When Bill had to expand, he moved his business into the downtown area of Reading—the building they occupy is listed on the National Historic Register and speaks to the cause they have identified as their philanthropic benefactor, urban renewal.

After being identified by *Inc.* magazine as the eighteenth fastest growing business within America's inner cities, Bill and his team know their commitment to downtown Reading has greater significance. Their future plans call for taking a leadership role in promoting healthy downtown districts beginning with their own.

In its own way, the mere existence of Bill's Khakis has been a minor American miracle. Somehow, the brand has managed to build a cult following in a market category so massive, it would reject the notion of a business that strives to sell and service one pair of khakis at a time.

It's an approach to business not found often anymore, and a

core element of their product's integrity. Of course, what people really want is simple: a good product they can count on.

But I think he has coupled that understanding with a memory: the memory that what we had as kids was a dream and a good pair of khakis.

The Best Room Service Ever

The first time my colleague David came to visit my studio in Philadelphia, he stayed at the Westin Liberty Place in downtown Philly, a very well-run hotel. When he called the desk to request a wake-up call, they said, "Would you like breakfast tomorrow morning?"

David doesn't usually eat breakfast, so he said, "No thanks. Just the wake-up call."

But the woman at the desk said, "Oh, we make very good omelettes, and we use only farm-fresh eggs."

It all goes back to Home Pride Buttertop Bread. Farm fresh? Where do the rest of them come from? Factories?

Always one to appreciate a good up-sell, David said, "Okay, yes, I'll have breakfast."

The next morning, David got his wake-up call and not three minutes later, a guy came to the door and wheeled in the breakfast cart with a stack of newspapers under his arm. The room-service guy pulled the reading chair around and fanned the newspapers out on the table and said, "What would you like to start with today, sir?'

He had the *Financial Times, The Wall Street Journal, The*

New York Times, the *Philadelphia Inquirer, USA Today*—far more than just the one newspaper you get by your door.

David said, "I'll start with *The New York Times* today." And the room-service guy said, "Why don't you get started on the paper while I get your food ready."

The room-service guy put out the orange juice, the coffee and the omelette. Then he pulled out a toaster from the bottom of the cart, took it over to the table and plugged it in.

David said, "Wow, this is amazing. I've never seen this before. Is this some kind of corporate policy?" And the room-service guy said, "No, sir. No policy. I bought that toaster myself and I bring it to work every day."

David asked if any of the other waiters brought toasters, and the waiter said, "No, sir. Just me."

Then the waiter opened up: "When I stay someplace and I order room service, the toast is always cold. I like hot toast. So I decided that the toast will never be cold, at least not on my watch."

He popped the toast out onto the plate and David said, "You just earned yourself a big tip."

But the room-service guy said, "Thank you, sir, but that's not why I do this. I just want to be the best room-service waiter you've ever had."

He put the plate of warm toast on David's plate, asked if there was anything else, and he was on his way.

The art of room service: That guy is the same kind of artist that my father was.

This is a man who does his job with pride, not because some general manager from some big-city corporation comes into the hotel and says, "Now, we're going to really dazzle them!"

The Westin Liberty Place is not a five-star hotel, it's just a very good hotel in Philadelphia. It doesn't cost a billion dollars a night—if you want to pay that kind of money, go to the Four Seasons.

But I'll bet you their room service doesn't arrive with a toaster.

The Art of Big Business

I don't want to gang up on malls or big business. I'm actually a fan of big business and malls. But I'm a champion of small business, which is where it all starts.

Bill Gates started in his garage. He's still a small business-man at heart, who still uses his dad's attorney for Microsoft business. But try to name someone in any business who has changed the world at a faster rate than Bill Gates. And it all came from an idea in a garage.

Another great business story is Wal-Mart. As we were traveling through the heartland on our bus trip toward the Rally for America, we were approaching St. Louis, Missouri. I picked up the *Rand McNally Atlas* and on the back was a full-page ad for Wal-Mart. It said: "Wal-Mart. Good. Works. Serving our customers, serving our community."

That's what Wal-Mart does. That's not hype, that's not just some positioning statement. All good positioning statements are real, they're true and they're verifiable. Wal-Mart *does* do good work. Wal-Mart *does* serve its customers. And Wal-Mart *does* serve its community. Now that my father is retired, all he wants to do is be a Wal-Mart greeter. He'd be great at it. The art of saying, "Welcome."

We are entering a time in American business when smart businessmen will know that if they create a situation in which everybody wins, they can make a lot more money.

If my customers win, if my community wins, if my employees win, I win.

If I can help improve the schools in a place where my factories are, I win in the long run. And I will win for a very long time.

People are dying for something real. We're living in a world where all we want is a politician to say, "Look, man, this is the way it is: I cheated on my wife. I made a mistake, but you know what? I have atoned for it, I have been forgiven by my wife, and I'm busting my butt to do the right thing by my family. I've made mistakes but I'm a better person today than I was yesterday because of those mistakes. And I'm not making the same mistakes over and over again."

We live in a world where people are yearning for that: "Just tell us the truth."

Companies like Wal-Mart that start to do more than simply position themselves, companies that start to walk the walk and live it are going to find their businesses exploding.

General Steel

Another client of mine on the radio program is General Steel, which builds steel buildings. Now, whenever an advertiser wants me to do commercials personally, it's important to me

that I meet them or use their product or at least have contact with their business. So when I heard about this company that builds steel buildings, my eyes immediately started to roll back into my head.

I couldn't imagine anything interesting about building steel buildings.

So I sat down with the owner, Jeff Knight, who told me this story of how he became General Steel.

Years ago Jeff was working for a company, and he was the top salesperson in the company. It was time for the yearly company awards, which they hand out at a big banquet, and this was a big deal for him. He was very excited, and his wife, Sherri, and his family were there. He walked up toward the podium to get the award, and he heard the CEO say to his manager, "What's this guy's name again?"

Jeff realized that he was the number one biller in this company and the guy at the top didn't even really know who he was. He went home and he sat down at the kitchen table with his wife. They had just moved into a brand new house—they had struggled for years to save up enough money to buy this big beautiful house, their dream house.

"Honey," he said to his wife, "Why am I doing this? Why am I working for somebody who doesn't even know my name? Why—when I could do it better? When I could treat my customers better? When I can make a better product myself?"

He sat there at the kitchen table and outlined his idea for a company to his wife, his first partner, and she said, "Honey—if you think we can really do it, let's do it."

And he said, "I tell you, we're going to have to sell this

house. I know we just moved in, I know we worked hard for this, but we won't be able to afford it. This is going to take every dime we've got."

So they sold the house and poured all of their money and all of his attention into what he called General Steel. It's now, years later, the number one steel-building manufacturer in the world. They sell buildings in Europe, England and Saudi Arabia; even our friends the French are buying them. All across America they're buying them too.

I'm not talking those little sheds you put in the backyard. I'm talking giant steel buildings.

When I heard him tell this story, I knew I wanted him as a client. Because here's a guy who doesn't have a college education, who just had a dream, who just had an idea that he could do it better.

He had the stick-to-itiveness and the courage to actually walk out on the ledge and take the jump.

By the way, Jeff knows the name of his top salesguy—and not just the night of the banquet, but all year-round.

A Company That Cares

Entrepreneurs and people who own their own businesses lead a hard, hard life. Believe me, I saw how my dad worked his whole life, and at seventy-five, he still doesn't own his own house outright. The reward is independence, but the price can be your whole life. That's why there are people who want to work for corporations and others who want to run them.

In the 1990s, corporations and the people who run them started to get horrible rap. Just ponder WorldCom—think of the scumbag who ran WorldCom into the ground. Think about Global Crossing and Enron. When you think of them, you think of the ultimate in corporate greed. You think about nothing but excess and that awful phrase: shareholder value.

Those are two words I never want to hear again in my life, because the ones who say "shareholder value" are usually the ones who don't have any interest at all in the value of the shareholders.

They're also usually the ones with all of the shares! And they're the ones who never learned the real definition of the word *share*.

But there are some companies that do it right, on a big scale. One of those companies is SAS, a data-warehousing innovator with revenues of $1.13 billion and nearly ten thousand employees in over one hundred offices worldwide.

SAS treats its employees the right way and they do that because it's good business. They treat their people the way they would want to be treated, and they spend a lot of money in ways that would seem extreme to someone who claims to be worried about "shareholder value."

They provide benefits ranging from having on-site medical care for their thousands of employees to providing country club memberships worth $10,000 available to SAS employees for $1,000. Employees can find services like dry cleaning and oil changes right there at work.

If you brought things like this up to the average CFO at a major corporation, he would tell you you're insane. "We don't do oil changes," he would say. "We make widgets." At SAS, they realize that by treating their people well and saving their people time, they are really putting those investment dollars back into the company.

The people who run SAS think out of the box: "Now, just hang on. . . . If we have an in-house doctor, there's no waiting room. There's no travel. If somebody's sick, they can get medical attention right away. We can cut down on the sick days. We can cut down on the half days for people to get to medical appointments. Hmmm . . . this could work."

If Sally Muckenfutch is sick, she calls the SAS doctor and asks, "What time can you squeeze me in?" The doctor says, "Three-thirty this afternoon, Sally." At 3:25 Sally gets a call at her extension. *Brrrr, rrrrr, rrrr!* "Sally, we're running a few minutes late. We'll call you when we're ready." They call at 3:45, Sally goes down, and there's no waiting.

The benefit to the employee: She doesn't have to go to a doctor and wait for an hour and a half.

The benefit to the company: The company doesn't have an employee wasting a whole day in a waiting room.

The way they run their company is important. They also have on-site, full-time artists, who produce art for the hallways. Try to tell stockholders how that's making them money, something as intangible as a pleasant workspace.

It's important to point out that SAS is a privately held company. The CEO was interviewed on *60 Minutes* and said he could never do this in a publicly owned and traded company. He said that if his company was public, and they got into a little trouble, the first thing to go would be the on-staff massage therapist. The next thing would be the full-time crew that helps staff members find the right colleges for their kids.

But as an employee, can you imagine how much time that would save?

It's also interesting to point out that SAS is in an industry with an employee turnover rate of more than 20 percent. SAS's turnover rate for the last ten years is 3 percent. The cost of training a new employee in the technology business is twenty thousand dollars. But having such a low turnover rate, they're actually saving millions of dollars by treating their employees like partners.

This is one of the models I'm using to build my company.

I'm actually a little hacked off at Spielberg, Geffen and Katzenberg for taking the name "Dreamworks" first, because that's really how I see my company. I want to find partners who dream big and understand that if we take their dream and couple it with my dream, we can be hugely successful and enrich each other's lives.

I used to think I could do it all myself. I used to be the biggest egomaniac in the world and thought that I had all the answers. Now that I'm thirty-nine and I've had a few hard knocks (such as losing my family, and all my money by the time I was thirty and bottoming out), I realize I have some skills and some huge deficits as well. There are things I cannot do, so I need to find partners who will be strong in the areas I am weak, even if they are weak in the areas I am strong.

Mercury Radio Arts

When I explain my vision for my media company, Mercury Radio Arts, I'm amazed at how many people, even industry leaders, ask me for a job. And I'm not even hiring yet. What captures their imagination is that MRA doesn't hire employees, it engages partners.

Radio is a business where someone in my position can make a ton of money every year and work side by side with someone making minimum wage. I think it's obscene to have that kind of earning potential and not spread the wealth with the people who help you to get there. So as I get to that place, my partners will share the earnings.

Nobody gets to the pinnacle of their profession with employees. You get to that level with partners. My partners are my wife, Tania; David Hall; Eric Chase; my COO/Dream Builder, Chris Balfe; my agent and trusted counsel, George Hiltzik; and my stunt brain, Steve Burguiere—you know him as Stu.

Let me give you a quick snapshot of what each of them does for me. Starting with my wife, Tania. I think you know what she does for me if you know what I mean (radio fans: mentally insert martini music here). The most important job in my career is done by Tania—I don't think she fully understands how vital it is yet, but she is the one who keeps me healthy—physically, mentally and, most important, spiritually. She keeps me rooted in all that is real.

David Hall is not an MRA partner, but his role is vital nonetheless. David is senior vice president of programming

for the Premiere Radio Networks, the company that syndicates my radio show along with Rush Limbaugh, Jim Rome and Dr. Laura. David helps me think. He is a master storyteller and helps me sift through the mundane to find the nuggets of talk-radio gold. One of his greatest strengths is his ability to think out of the box, not as a radio programmer, but as a listener.

Eric Chase is a production genius who should be working for Skywalker Sound. He's an audio dreamer. He currently is responsible for all of our theme songs and is quintessential partner material. I never have to tell Eric how to adjust our show's imaging. I usually only have to tell him what I want something to feel like and he returns with brilliance. In an employee/employer relationship, people like Eric become frustrated and disenfranchised because people like me, who are far less talented in the employee's area of expertise, try to micromanage.

The same can be said for my relationship with Chris Brady, who has built what I believe to be the best website, bar none, www.glennbeck.com. Every year we redesign the look of the site. And, again, with Chris I only tell him what I want it to feel like and he takes it from there.

Chris Balfe is the partner I call when I have a dream. He's the guy who enables me to stay focused on the show and the big picture. He sees my vision the first time and gets it done. He also has a natural ability to see structure, pattern and the route to a finished product. As my COO, he ties all of the creative pieces together and keeps us functioning as one.

Now, it could be said that my agent and management partner, George Hiltzik, is the anti-Chris. I often tell him he's a *Columbo* episode in which all the murderers get away. His disarming mannerisms could make one believe he only sees the vision on the eighth rewrite. Don't let his crumpled raincoat fool you. He is usually the smartest guy in the room and six months ahead of everyone else. He knows how big business thinks, he has the right connections and he is a master at the art of the deal.

And finally, Stu. He started with me as an intern. He is now one of my most trusted partners and the best comedy writer in radio today. Stu is responsible for writing and producing all of the comedy bits on *The Glenn Beck Program*. I am convinced that when the talents of Eric and Stu are combined, try as they may, radio shows will not be able to replicate their comedic product for years to come.

Each of these individuals has a strength where I have a weakness. The most important attribute in a Mercury partner is that they are all good people first. When your team has trust and respect coupled with talent, you can change the world. And this team is about to do that.

Why Steve Is Called Stu
(For Dedicated Listeners Only)

I first met Stu through a guy who was writing for my show who I think was heavily intoxicated at the time. Stu and I met at a bar, and his name—Steve—was somehow slurred during transition so badly I thought it was Stu. Over the coming months I kept calling Steve "Stu" and he never corrected me. He thought, "Oh, it's just Glenn. He lives in his own world, and if it makes him happy that in his world my name is Stu . . . what does it matter? He's a complete loser has-been anyway."

So this went on for several months. Later we became friends (yes, I have a couple of them) and I wanted him to intern and eventually produce for my show. This put Stu/Steve in a precarious position. "Do I tell 'Glenn the oblivious' he's been calling me the wrong name for months? Or do I just leave it alone?"

One day, we are on the air and I was grasping for something to make fun of Stu about. So I said:

GLENN: Well, that name—Stu: what is that? Is that a family name? Like Stuart?"

STU: Glenn, my name's not Stu.
  I paused. This was on the air—live.

GLENN: What do you mean your name's not Stu?

STU: My name's not Stu. It's Steve.

GLENN: So how come I've been calling you Stu this whole time?

STU: Glenn, I just don't know—you just started calling me Stu the first day. And I just didn't care enough to stop you.

Well, Stu should have cared. To this day, I call him Stu on and off the air. But it's not just me. His wife Lisa, whom he met after this conversation, also calls him Stu.

The name "Mercury Radio Arts" comes from Orson Welles's Mercury Radio Theater. I have enormous respect for Orson Welles the dreamer, not Orson Welles the person. Welles destroyed himself by allowing his ego to trap him in his past. He lost sight of what *could be* and focused on what *could have been*—which is why a man who possessed one of the most uniquely creative minds of the century ended up begging friends for money while doing card tricks and died penniless.

But before he lost his way, he performed what I would call *real* magic. He not only produced and directed, but he designed the costumes and sets and starred in *Macbeth* with the first all-black cast in the 1930s. It was his first success. Here's a guy in his early twenties who was in such demand on Broadway and on radio that he would do a radio show before his Broadway matinee, then go do another broadcast in between the two Broadway shows.

His problem quickly became that there wasn't enough time in the day for him to get from one place to the other. One day he was walking on the street with his partner, John Houseman, and they were talking about this very problem when an ambulance went by with its sirens blazing. Welles stopped dead in his tracks and said to Houseman, "I want you to find out if you actually have to be sick to ride in one of those things."

Houseman found out that you didn't *have* to be sick, so Welles hired an ambulance to pick him up from the Broadway show, turn the sirens on, and take him to CBS, where he played a role on the radio. Then they would pack him back in the ambulance, turn the sirens on again and go back to the Broadway theater to do the second show.

This guy didn't understand the word *no*. There was a way to create *anything*. Welles inspires me to believe that I can create anything that I can see or imagine. I just have to find ways around the natural obstacles, from having enough time in the day, to a company's "no police." I just have to think out of the box.

So what we're going to do with Mercury Radio Arts is create a company full of dreamers, who believe that there's more to entertainment companies then just selling advertising. And maybe if I'm lucky my kids will remember my love for radio art like I remember my father's love for his art.

Let me show you our idea in practice in hopes you will be able to apply the thinking to your business art. A great company philosophy that inspires us at Mercury Radio Arts comes from Live Planet Productions, Matt Damon and Ben Affleck's company. These guys are brilliant. They did something called Project Greenlight that started with the great old concept, "Hey, let's make a movie."

Then they took it to the next level. They decided that they wanted to have a screenwriting contest, conducted on their website. People submitted their scripts to the site and then returned often to see what scripts were in the running, which had been read, etc. Audience was constantly flowing to the site to keep up.

Now they had two entertainment products and two sources of revenue, the movie and the website.

But they also said, "You know, this whole process is very interesting. We should go to HBO and ask them to make a documentary on the making of this."

When it was all over, they packaged the whole thing into a set of DVDs, including all the behind-the-scenes gossip involved in the website, the movie and the TV show.

That's four. Four distinct forms of entertainment, four ways to reach their audience, four products that act as marketing and publicity for each other and four sources of revenue.

You can probably guess what I said the first time I heard this concept: "That doesn't suck." And I was right. It sucks so little, in fact, that the next season of Project Greenlight is going on right now. What will they think of this time?

Whatever it is, we plan to be two steps ahead of them. This is what Mercury Radio Arts aspires to be in the world of radio. We want to start with *The Glenn Beck Program* and find ways to maximize its impact in the community while at the same time maximizing its ratings and revenue.

Sound interesting? While we're not currently hiring, we're always taking applications. If you have a business dream or a love for radio, please submit your application online at www.glennbeck.com.

But it's important to us that we don't build our company on greed. We can find six more ways to get people to spend more money, but for our company to really succeed, we must not only provide the highest quality products, but also be responsible with its profits. That's the seed of the idea: enrich all, not just those at the top. And one of its early buds is that over 10 percent of everything MRA earns goes to charity. I encourage my partners to do the same.

One of the dreams and goals of my company is that, at some point, we will have a CCO: a chief charitable officer, some-

body who will oversee how we can impact our community and help not only our employees and our partners, but also those around us.

An Enlightened Way to Wealth

I know, you just bought this book, but go back to the bookstore and buy another one. It's called *The One-Minute Millionaire: The Enlightened Way to Wealth*. Robert Allen and Mark Victor Hansen's concept is that it's not just about you, and it's not just about getting rich. It's about enriching yourself, your life, the other people around you and the lives of the people in your community.

If I'm rich, everybody on my staff should be wealthy as well.

This might sound counterintuitive, because it's very easy in today's society to become very, very greedy. But the reason I believe this and know this to be true is that my faith has a concept called "tithing."

In my faith we believe that God said, "Prove me. I will open up the windows of Heaven and more blessings will flow into your house that it will not to be able to hold all of them." That's quite a promise. All I'm supposed to do to deserve that is give away 10 percent of my earnings. That's it. Okay, I'm being sarcastic. That's a lot if you don't believe the promise.

So I decided to test the promise because I wanted enough blessings for my house not to be able to hold all of them, so I began tithing, giving my 10 percent. The great thing about promises from God, if you do specifically what He asks, He has to follow through on His promise or He ceases to be God.

Well, my life changed. I know people can easily make fun of tithing as if it's some cliché like, "Oh, my car broke down and I couldn't afford to fix it, but I gave away my 10 percent and whaddya know? I found the money to fix my car! It always works out like that when I tithe."

You hear things like that and it starts to sound like a Charlie Brown teacher: *"Brraaaap-br-brap braaappp brap brap."* (My editor Mitchell loves that line.)

But I'm telling you that once you commit to giving away your 10 percent you will get so much more back. And the reason for that is that *it's not your money.* Money and riches are just things that you are the steward of.

So if you believe in an anthropomorphic God, you believe that the Lord is saying to you, "I'm going to give you this money and let's see what you do with it. And if you do good things with it, I'm going to give you more."

But there's another way to look at it, for those of you who don't believe in God. (Hello, California: Ladies, in your sandals, with your unshaven armpits, eating granola, this is for you.) There are certain truths in the universe that appear in many religions, one of which is: *As you believe, so shall it be.*

Here's how this universal principle works with tithing: If I am busy protecting my money, if I am busy hoarding my money, if I am busy trying to make sure that my employees only get as much as they *need* because I think that *I* need that money, what I'm creating in my life is simply *my need.* I'm creating my own shortages.

But if I pay my employees, if I take care of them, if I spread my money around wisely, if I'm not *afraid* of spending that money, I will know that by helping them they'll help me, that I will have enough money to go around, and I will without fail create wealth in my own life and the lives of others. There will be enough money to go around.

What kills me are people who feel like they need to hoard money because there is not enough. There is a universe full of money. There are riches beyond your wildest dreams. God doesn't give you a taste of ice cream unless he's willing for you to have the whole cone.

It's interesting to me that Jesus said, "Inside my Father's house there are many mansions." He didn't call it a little hovel; he didn't say it was a cave. He said, "There is a mansion for you." That means that wealth and riches are not bad things. It's not the wealth, it's what you do with it. They are things that everyone should have, and they are things that everyone can have. God believes you deserve a mansion. Do you?

CHAPTER 10

Glenn Beck: Behind the Music

In my wallet I used to carry an extra driver's license. It was my grandfather's.

His name was Edward Janssen, and he was a mountain of a man, or at least he seemed so to me. I would stay with my grandparents every summer and work on their farm. It was the kind of place where if you didn't finish your supper, the plate would wait for you on top of the refrigerator till morning.

I remember Grandpa with his calloused hands and Grandma with her can of bacon grease. Ed and Clara Janssen were hard-working people from Iowa. No nonsense, practical, God-fearing and warm, they were part of what has become known as the greatest generation, forged in the fires of the Great Depression.

As a man, he really wasn't that much of a mountain. Now I

am four inches taller than he was. But I carry his driver's license with me as a reminder of the man I admired and loved, to remind myself that I also carry with me something that has been woven over time into the very fabric of who I am. It is the part of him that was genuine: his strength, his decency and his belief in the inherent goodness of America.

I have had the driver's license since he died, but I have only recently come into possession of those other qualities. As I grew up, as most young people do, I decided my grandparents were quaint, old-fashioned and different from me. While I always loved them, I outgrew them. I no longer wanted to be like my grandparents, because the world had changed, people had changed and quite frankly their life seemed boring.

My grandfather had an old tool box he built by hand. It must have been fifty years old when he died. The tool box was made of wood, and it was heavy, sturdy and durable. He never wanted a new one, and he had no interest in the latest tool box. The one he built by hand was good enough to last his whole life.

As I travel further from my childhood and the excesses of my twenties, I find myself yearning for the strength, the courage and the simplicity of my grandparents, but especially for their faith.

One Man's Spiritual Journey

What you are going to read may make you think that I am totally insane.

You may relate to it, or you may not. You may think it's the wrong path, or you may think it's the right path. I'm not trying to change you. This is one man's spiritual journey and let's leave it at that.

I had a friend over at my house recently, and she said, "Glenn, you once said something to me that helped me chart a new course." I said "Really? Tell me what it was—maybe it will help *me*." She showed me what I said, which she had scrawled in a notebook: *Application of your faith will change your life*.

I joked, "If I had known you were going to remember it, I probably would have worked on it a bit. I mean, I could dress it up a little, make it a bit more profound." But she told me it was fine just the way it was.

Application of your faith will change your life. Gee, I wish I could have given myself that little bumper-sticker hogwash ten years ago. Maybe I wouldn't have gone though all I did. You know, it's easy for me to say those things now, but unfortunately, it took me up until four years ago just to find what I had faith in.

When I was eight years old my mom gave me an album called *The Golden Years of Radio*. I became mesmerized by what magic radio was, how it could create pictures in my head. I got my first radio job, believe it or not, when I was thirteen years old. I got fired. I got fired from three jobs in one day. But by the time I was eighteen years old, I was programming as well as doing the morning show on a station that would go from worst place to first place in my first ratings period.

As a kid who had been on the radio his whole high school

career with people referring to me as a wunderkind, my ego was a little out of control. By the time I was in my twenties, I was extremely successful, and as far as I was concerned, I had everything. However, the people in my neighborhood must have thought I was some kind of crack dealer. They didn't know who I was, and they didn't listen to my show. I was twenty-five years old and had limo service everywhere. I never really seemed to be at work, because I did a four-hour show. So my neighbors thought, "What does this guy do for a living . . . and are my kids safe?"

Yes, you would think I had everything and in material wealth you may have been right. But I also had this wacky thing going for me called alcoholism. Over time I have found that I am actually allergic to alcohol because when I drink it, I break out in insanity.

The more money I received, the more miserable I became because the clothes and the cars weren't making me happy. I kept thinking, "Jeez, I should really be high as a kite—look at this car I just bought—it's my dream car. I *better* be happy now." I was for a few days and then it started all over again.

So I started to drink.

Actually I started really drinking hard when I took a month off and went to Italy. *Never* spend a month in Italy. I went to Italy and gained probably 450 pounds on a diet that consisted of nothing but pasta and booze. I hated red wine before I went to Italy, but soon after arriving there, I found I loved it. I started to drink red wine the way I used to drink water. I could have cut out everything else—milk, water, soda, meat—and lived on red wine.

There was a point there where I think I actually may have had too much blood in my red wine system.

And that's where I discovered that, hey, you know what? Wine and booze make the pain go away. Not that I had more pain than you or anybody else—I mean, we all have crap to deal with. We all have stories of tragic, horrible things that have happened to us, like somebody stomping on our hearts, or telling us how bad we were. Everybody has something like that: same basic story, different surroundings and different names—that's the only difference.

But I needed to kill my pain. Actually, what I needed to do was stop *thinking* about my "stories." This is when I met my good friend and physician for many years: Dr. Jack Daniel's.

"Paging Dr. Daniel's, Dr. Jack Daniel's to Glenn Beck's house STAT."

Jack and I had a long and luscious relationship. Oh yeah, Dr. Jack would nurse me to sleep night after drunken night after drunken night.

By the time I was thirty, I was a mess. I was working at a small radio station in Connecticut. I hadn't worked in a market that small since I was fifteen years old. I hated it, and I was miserable. I was running three stations for Clear Channel but as anyone who was there at the time will tell you, I was basically running them into the ground.

My motto was "I hate people." People who knew me back then see me now and are astonished, because they actually like me and I like them. I'm the guy who used to hate them, who thought they were a waste of time, thought they were all sniveling, worthless idiots. If I wanted something done right I would do it myself.

I hated people because I hated myself.

That was what got me into the 102nd largest market in the country. There's nothing like being eighteen years old in the fifth largest market in America, and then spending the next dozen years dropping ninety-seven spots.

"Paging Dr. Daniel's, Dr. Jack Daniel's."

"I'm coming brother, relax."

It was the eve of my thirtieth birthday, and I'd lost everything. I'd lost my money. I'd lost my fancy car. And I was about to lose my family.

I can remember the dance of the numbers on the digital clock. Have you ever noticed that sometimes if you stare at a digital clock the numbers will kind of float and move around a bit? I remember seeing them almost dance at what was to come.

The numbers said 11:59 and it was February 9. I whispered to myself, "My life is about to change."

Then it turned 12:00, February 10, and I was thirty.

That was 1994. By the end of 1994 I was sober—no, I was what they call a "dry drunk."

I actually stopped drinking in November 1994, at a fundraiser. I had to be there for three days, twenty-four hours a day raising money for hungry children.

I thought I could do that: three days, *whew,* that's not so bad.

Only my best friends knew I was going through DTs. But I was a crazy man that weekend: "Hey, little kid, you want to come over here and meet me? I'm Glenn Beck—you listen to me on the radio and *I've got spiders all over my face! Aaar-rrggghhh!"*

That was the last time I had a drink, right before Thanksgiving 1994. It's an amazing thing when you actually have the courage to stand up, maybe only because you've been so beaten down, and admit that you are an alcoholic to a room full of drunks.

I thought to myself, "What am I *doing* here? You're all *drunks*. Why am I even talking to you people? If you guys had a clue, you wouldn't all be *drunks*."

But I stood up in that room and I was embarrassed. I said: "Hello my name is Glenn, and I am not sure I am an alcoholic. I just know that I don't want to drink today, and I can't do it alone." (Gee, Glenn, do you think not being able to stop drinking might be a sign that you are an alcoholic?)

I really didn't want to admit that I needed to go to AA. I think it was because I thought the members were . . . well, drunks. When I arrived in that little church basement in Cheshire, Connecticut, on that Sunday, I thought I might be in the wrong room. These people didn't *look* like drunks . . . they looked like *me*. By the end of that first meeting, I stood up and reintroduced myself: "Hello my name is Glenn and I *am* an alcoholic."

I thought the worst part would be standing there in that room full of people and admitting to them and to myself that I had a drinking problem. But, it wasn't. The worst part was finding out what made me need to self-medicate.

I began to work the program and do some of the twelve

steps, and it didn't take long before I knew I was on the threshold of something profound. Something that would either heal or kill me. It was the black abyss of what had become my sense of self and all that I had done or thought. These were the reasons I drank: I was terrified and ready to die at the empty end of a bottle rather than probe any deeper in the shadows of my soul.

Until one night. I had a dream. I actually believe that it was more of a personal prompting than just a dream. In fact, I woke up at three in the morning and had to sit down and paint a picture because this dream was so vivid and its message so clear. There are probably five or six real turning points in my life and while most of them happened in a tight two- or three-year period, this is the one that started it all rolling.

In this dream I'm standing at the end of a road and on each side of me are these broken stalks, a cornfield, in the middle of winter. There is just a little bit of snow, so you can still see the brown of the dirt. Everything in the picture I painted was brown and dark and dead. I painted the road the way I remembered it, going all the way down to the horizon, perfectly flat.

The sky above and around the sides of me was that cloudy gray kind of cold winter white sky. But in front of me, right at the end of the roadway, it was black—and I mean black-hole black.

When I woke up, I tried to paint the black hole, but I couldn't get the black black enough. I remember pushing the brush hard into the canvas, trying to get it blacker, and I couldn't.

That black I saw was almost like velvet black. It absorbed all of the light and I felt that it was calling to me. In the dream, I'm standing there thinking, "Okay, well, I'm not going down this road."

There was no other road around and I thought, "Well, I'll just have to stand here. This is where I'm hanging out because I can't go through that 'storm.'"

Then an old man came up next to me, all in tattered clothing and really dingy and dirty with a big kind of grayish beard—again, everything was gray or brown—and he whispered, "You must walk through it."

I replied, "Oh, no, I can't."

He whispered again, "You gotta walk down this road."

More firmly now I fired back, "No. I can't! It will kill me."

He smiled, "Really, there's nothing to be afraid of."

"No."

"Glenn, go through it."

I stood there for a while, my fear palpable.

That's when he grabbed my hand and softly said, "Come with me."

Now, I don't know how we got to the other side—it was kind of like "Hey, I'm Peter Pan." I think we flew all the way around the road and arrived at the other side of the dark cloud.

Now I was *facing* the dark cloud, looking at the back of it, and it was still velvet black but the road started to come out, almost like the yellow brick road in *The Wizard of Oz*. The road was clean, but I remember that everything on this side was lush and green and beautiful. And he said, "This is what's

on the other side." When I looked over at him, he was dressed all in white and his hair was pure white, almost like fiber optics—light was coming out of the ends of each strand.

And I looked at him and he said, "This *is* the other side. There's nothing in between. It's just the fear that stops you from going through it. It's warm and beautiful here. Walk through the storm, I will wait here."

That was the last thing he said to me. Then I found myself on the other side of the cloud, back on the dirty side with the dead corn stalks, snow and bitter temperatures, and that's when I woke up. I still have that painting, I keep it in the back of one of my closets, just to remind me of what things looked like before I stepped shakily, blinking into the sun.

When I started to do the twelve steps of AA, I started to catalog all the horrible things that I had been keeping inside of me. Once, after I had taken my personal inventory, as the twelve steps call it, somebody asked me on the air, "Hey, did you ever do such and such?"—in a kind of an accusing tone, like, "Yeah, yeah, Mr. High and Mighty—you're telling me you've *never* done this?"

Everybody in the room expected me to say, "Hmmm, no, I never have." But at that point in my life, I was more than ready to end my career, so I said, "Uh . . . yeah. *Yeah!* I have; I've done a lot of bad things." Everybody in the room and everyone in the audience was dumbfounded. Stu was my producer at the time, and I said, "Stu, write this date down: This is the day Glenn Beck ended his career."

And you know what? Just the opposite happened. It's so true: The truth *will* set you free. That was the day I started to *do* real radio, because I wasn't hiding anything. And the audience embraced it—because they felt I was saying, "I'm just like you and you're just like me. We've *all* done horrible things."

When the audience discovered that I didn't think that I was perfect, and that I would admit my faults and problems, we started to have a real dialogue. It's not that they held me in higher esteem, I think they just thought more highly of themselves. They thought, "Oh well, holy cow. Well, I've done *that*." Or "I'm better off than that guy—what a loser he is!"

What this dream taught me is this: Digging up the past and examining your faults won't kill you—it will cure you. There is a place of real warmth and beauty beyond description waiting for you just over the horizon.

But I need to back up a bit. . . .

God Is Stalking Me

I grew up Catholic, although my father was not a Catholic. He was a member of the Church of Religious Science, which was a granola-California, deeply philosophical, thinking man's kind of church. My father made a promise to my mother when they got married. He said, "I can't be a Catholic." And my mother said, "Well, we can't get married unless you promise me that our children will be Catholic." He did what any man of real integrity would do when faced with the thought of a honeymoon: He said, "Okay."

Funny, because when I met my wife, Tania, she said, "We have to find a church or we're not going to get married."

"Okay."

It's a thing that women do to men: "You'll go to church, and you'll like it." Yes, ma'am!

My dad kept his promise even after my mother's death. My sisters and I were raised Catholic, and we went to Catholic school for many years. It worked for me for awhile. But I really believe that God has been on a quest for my soul or attention for most of my life. He's been hunting me, with little traps like Wile E. Coyote's Acme road holes.

God has been stalking me. But God doesn't use Acme road holes, He uses people. And boy, the "snag Glenn recruiting office" must have been open late the night of my birth because His fingerprints have been all over so many people in my path.

When I was eighteen, I moved to Salt Lake City. Having grown up in a small farming community in Washington State, I didn't know a thing about Mormons except that Donny and Marie were members, they didn't drink coffee and Donny could have as many wives as he wanted. I found out later that they indeed are members and don't drink coffee but there can only be *one Mrs. Donny Osmond.* Until the company I worked for transferred me to Salt Lake City, I had never even met a Mormon.

This is where the Lord started to lay His traps for me.

I was living in nearby Provo, so it was just a lot of Mormons and me. The first day I went to the radio station—remember, I'm just eighteen and clean-cut—I pulled out a cigarette and everybody said, "Oh . . . I thought you were Mormon." And I said, "Oh . . . I thought you were normal."

I was only making about $12 a year, so I had to have a roommate. Of course I ended up rooming with a returned Mormon missionary.

The Lord's hot breath was right there on the back of my neck. As it turns out, it was more like I was turning him to the dark side than him turning me. What a surprise, within six months, I was transferred to WPGC in Washington, D.C.

So I am away from the Mormons, or so I think. The guy I now work with, J. Robert Howe, the newsman at the station, turns out to be another Mormon. I develop a friendship with him, and we work together for about six months. He was a really great guy, but I got in with a bad crowd and started making friends with some seriously screwed-up individuals. After a while, I began to turn on my Mormon friend, wanting him to fail. And, lo and behold, I found myself fired.

Now this story could be about God stalking me, or it could be a master disguise for a story that just says, "I can't seem to hold a job."

I found myself out of work and for months I searched for a new station that was hiring. I couldn't find anything. Desperate, I finally found a job in Corpus Christi, Texas, where I was the program director and the morning guy on a small radio station. It was a good job—I was the boss. . . . Well, there was one other guy above me and he was . . . a Mormon.

At this point I started to think, "Holy cow, can we stop with the Mormon stuff? How many Mormons *are* there? Every place I go there's another Mormon!"

I held on to that job in Texas for two years and then moved to various cities, eventually ending up in Baltimore, Maryland. I had been talking with Michael Opelka, a writer/pro-

ducer at Z100 in New York City, for several years about doing a show together. He had written for several national shows and was just about the funniest guy I ever met. Michael and I had put this show together but at the last minute it fell through and he stayed in NYC.

I now had only five days to put the show on, and it was one of the most important shows I ever had to do. I needed a partner, I needed a writer, and I had nothing.

I started calling everybody I knew. Finally somebody said, "Glenn, I know the perfect talent. You guys would sound great together. He's brilliant, he's funny. He's everything you need. You are going to love him professionally, but you are going to hate him personally."

I said, "Please, don't tell me he's a Mormon . . ."

He was.

I picked him up at the airport, and by the time we left the parking lot—we were best friends.

That's Pat Gray, my friend. We've been best friends now for fifteen years.

My Friend Pat

Much like the returned missionary, Pat doesn't watch R-rated movies. He doesn't drink. He doesn't smoke. I remember during my darkest hour—which possibly became his—I convinced Pat to go see *The Silence of the Lambs*.

Pat had not been to an R-rated movie in years. His church encourages members to seek out things that uplift and inspire, and Hannibal Lecter, as crazy as it seems, just doesn't do that. He said, "Glenn, I hear this is supposed to be really brutal." But I said, "No, I saw it last weekend and it really wasn't that bad."

I loved horror stuff, so I really didn't see a problem with it. I remember looking at him halfway through the movie, and all the blood was drained from his face. "You don't think *this* is bad?" he whispered.

"Well, I didn't notice it the first time around, I guess I am now seeing it through your eyes and, yeah, it is kind of dark, huh?" It was the same feeling you get when you are watching TV with your kids and a commercial with Sarah Jessica Parker comes on touting the last season of *Sex and the City* now with orgasms in "Sensurround." You probably didn't think twice the first time you saw it, okay maybe the orgasm part, but now you're seeing it through your kids' eyes. Pat and I, it was clear, had different background noise. Things were very quiet and decent in his world. That was the last R-rated movie he saw.

You're welcome, Pat.

When Pat and I really started to get to know each other, I really was a truly despicable human being. I was the bottom of my barrel. I will never forget the look on Pat's face when I told him I fired one of our producers because he brought me the wrong pen.

Part of the producer's job was to pick me up in a limousine and take me to malls for signings. I'd get out and say to the producer, "See that man over there? The guy who's paying me a thousand dollars for an hour to sit here and sign autographs? Your job is to keep him *away* from me." Then I would say to

the line of fans, "Hey! How you doing? Really great to see you," sign the autographs and move on.

I really hated people and I think most of those in line could tell.

I said to Pat, "You'll never believe this, this new producer we got? Two weeks ago I told him I need a Sharpie. Well, Saturday, when I went to sign autographs, he handed me a *regular ballpoint pen again.* So I fired him."

Pat had that same *Silence of the Lambs* look on his face, looking at me like I had just eaten the kid's kidneys. I thought I was perfectly reasonable. I mean—*I needed a Sharpie!* I didn't need the skin dress and the pit in my basement to be a monster. But Pat stood by me; I think he knew that the problem wasn't really that I hated people. The problem was I hated myself.

Once, I was slobbering drunk and said to him, "Heyyyyyy, Patsssshhh. I am looking for some *answers* I mean there's got to be more than just this." Pat got real quiet and said simply, "Well, you know, Glenn, I've got some answers."

"Ohhhhhhh no," I slurred back at him, "I don't wanna hear *those* answers." Of course not. Those answers required commitment and application of what you believed.

Pat would answer that question from me the same way every time I would ask it for many, many years and when rejected not preach or bring it up again. What a gentle man and good friend. I, on the other hand . . .

What Pat didn't know was that I was secretly wishing for Pat to fail, just as I wished for the returned missionary and the newsman at the station in Washington to fail. Because if their religion couldn't be lived properly by *them,* well then, somehow or another I was okay. But if they succeeded, if their families remained stable and close, if their principles kept them on course and helped them weather storms I could not, then I would probably have to take a look at it myself. And man, I didn't want to . . . no booze, no cigarettes and no more than one wife? That just wasn't me.

Soon enough, all that hate and self-hate caught up with me. I lost everything. I lost my family. I lost my job. I lost my money. I lost my sense of who I was.

I found myself standing in that room, in the basement of that church, saying, "Hello, my name is Glenn and I am an alcoholic. Help me."

AA helped me to deal with some of the stuff that caused me to hate myself. And as I started to help myself, I started to investigate other things. A year or so after I started going to AA meetings, I realized I still had some big questions I needed to answer for myself. You know, like what the meaning of life was . . . that kind of thing.

So I started looking for God—kind of. Not really. I don't know if I was really looking for Him because if I did, He might have actually asked me to do stuff. And Geez, I don't want celestial homework for the love of Pete. I was looking for truth *in theory.*

Now I'm a rather cheesy science-minded person. I like to read Stephen Hawking, I like to read Einstein, although it took me two and half years to read one of Einstein's books. But I fancied myself—and maybe this is from my dad—a very logical person.

As I was searching, I read a letter written by Thomas Jefferson to his nephew Peter Carr. Peter had lost his mother and his father. His mother died first, and when his father was gravely ill, he went to Jefferson and said, "Thomas, you're the smartest man I know. Please educate my son. Promise me that you will teach him and bring him to what he will need to know." Jefferson agreed, and when Peter Carr came of age—I think he was sixteen—Jefferson wrote him a letter that said, "Dear Peter," and I am paraphrasing Jefferson's elegant eloquence, "your father told me I am to teach you everything you need to know. In Mathematics, you need to read these books. In Philosophy, you need to understand this. In Languages, you need to know these languages." When he came to literature, he said that you should never read a book out of its native tongue because you will lose too much in the translation. Riiiiight.

Jefferson went through all of the studies, and at the very end he came to religion. "And above all things," he wrote, "when it comes to religion, fix reason firmly in her seat and question everything. Take no man's singular opinion. Question the very existence of God, *for if there be a God, He must surely rather honest questioning over blindfolded fear.*"

"Honest questioning over blindfolded fear": That phrase was a revelation for me. It was truth. Those are the words that brought me to a personal relationship with my Heavenly Father.

Why I Am a Mormon

Growing up Catholic in my family, there were questions you don't ask because "the devil is making you question this" or you'd get my favorite answer: "It's a mystery." Now in my thirties, I realized that I really didn't know God at all on a personal level. I only believed in God because someone told me He existed. And I was no longer afraid of questioning.

I wish I were the president, just for the 747 and the cabinet I could assemble. I would have the best minds that I could find with a special eye out for those people who would vehemently disagree with each other. I'd let them argue it out and just listen. Well, I'm not the president so the jet doesn't take off when I tell it to and I can't hire great minds to argue.

So, I did the next best thing, I drove to the bookstore. Here is who I put on my "book cabinet": I got Alan Dershowitz. He's opinionated, obnoxious and at times— when he's not talking about the OJ Simpson case—he makes a good point. Let's see, let's put him in a room with . . . Adolf Hitler. I'd love to see those guys go at it. So next: Hitler's *Mein Kampf.* Then something by Pope John Paul, along with Carl Sagan. I really looked hard, who else would I like to see in a room together? Hey, how about Nietzsche and Billy Graham? Yeah!

I thought it all made sense and was cool until I got to the checkout counter. I will never forget the look on the woman's face or her comments as she scanned the bar codes "Oh! Alan Dershowitz! That's a great book. *(Boop!)* Okay, Pope John

Paul *(boop)!* . . . and Nietzsche . . . interesting. *(Boop!)* . . . Adolf Hitler . . . Uh . . . *(boop!)* Thank you!"

As I saw the freakish collection of titles pass through this woman's hands I realized that I was assembling the library of a serial killer! This is what Hannibal Lecter reads. I began to imagine that the FBI databanks were being alerted as to my location. "Oh, one more thing, do you have a copy of *The Catcher in the Rye?*"

Meanwhile, my quiet little friend Pat was still saying, "Glenn, if you're looking for answers I have some for you."

"No thanks, Pat! You Mormons are freaks!"

Really? Which sick freak is reading *Mein Kampf?*

First to speak on my book council was Carl Sagan, who's an atheist. He took organized religion apart, and did it very well. He talked about the power and the manipulation and the greed, and I said to myself, "Now, there's a point of view I've never really considered. I've never considered *atheism*. Maybe there is no God. Maybe I'll try this on." That's the kind of world I live in. I try things on. I immerse myself in things, then pick them apart from the inside.

So I tried on atheism. I said to God, "I don't know if you exist. I do know, however, that if you really were our 'Father in Heaven' that you would leave breadcrumbs for your children to find their way back. Why would you erase your tracks. If you exist, I will find you, because you would want me to find you."

My path, my spiritual journey ended up taking me to Yale. There were too many questions that I couldn't figure out without some kind of structured study.

> Questions Glenn Thought an Ivy League Education
> Could Answer:
>
> - Why is it all the food I like is bad for you?
> - Why aren't there any conservative professors?
> - Why is sappy music called "elevator music," yet I
>   have never been in an elevator with music?

I took a class called Early Christology: The making of the image of Christ. The class was full of eighteen- and nineteen-year-old kids far smarter than I was, who were just trying to keep the teacher talking so they could skate through an easy course. I was thirty-two and trying to understand the meaning of life.

I was a very popular student. No one could keep the teacher talking longer than I could. One time while answering a question about the Resurrection, he told me that my thinking was in line with Dominic Crossan and the members of the "Jesus Seminar." I had never heard of them. Even though he told me not to read them because they were wrong and it would take me in the wrong direction . . . I went back to the bookstore. "Ladies and gentlemen of the cabinet, I would like to you meet Dominic Crossan. Dominic, Adolf. Adolf, Dominic."

A week later, after a few more questions, my professor looked at me with disbelief and said, "You've been reading Crossan even though I told you not to."

"Yes, sir," I replied, "I wanted to know *why* you disagreed with him." He told me later over lunch.

What I never told him was that not only did I read Crossan's book, I spent about two hours on the phone with him. My professor was right: Crossan is *wrong*.

When we began to study the making of the Trinity, I remember sitting there in class thinking, "Am I the only one who thinks this doesn't work? They just took all this stuff and crammed it together for political reasons, edited the Bible where it would contradict the profession of faith and said, 'There it is. There is the essence of God!' Then they killed everyone who disagreed with them. Am I the only one?"

I mentioned this to Pat and once again he said quietly, "Glenn, if you want some answers, I have some for you." Not interested, Freak Boy.

Then I met Tania. Women have this way of changing a man's life. Tania told me about a year into dating: "If you want to marry me, we have to go to church." I would rather listen to Barbra Streisand talk politics while surrounded by cats. Actually, what she said was even sneakier: "You know, Glenn, your children really don't *know* God."

"What do you mean?" I asked her. "We talk about God all the time. I'm searching for Him, baby! First of all, I'm a dad. You don't even *have* kids, so back off!"

Women love it when you talk down to them.

She said, "Glenn, I will make a bet with you that your kids are not God-centered. If you asked them what their family was based on they would *never* say God." I took the bet.

Three reasons never to go to Vegas with me:

1. I'm an alcoholic.
2. I'm a Mormon.
3. I'd lose all your money.

That Saturday night we went to what should have been the gaming tables at Jerry Iannacone's Polo Grille in New Haven, our favorite restaurant. I was cocky because "I know my kids." We sat down and I said, "Kids, let's talk."

I started to make a list. They had no idea what was going on: just a little conversation with Dad with a pencil and paper. I said, "Kids, you know what we're going to talk about: What makes us our family? What's our family all about? What are we centered on? Anything at all comes to mind?" Here it comes, I'm thinking: GOD.

I wrote their answers down. I have it in my wallet with Grandpa's license.

Coming in at Number 1: *fun*. Okay, all right. God is fun. Tania? No.

"Okay kids, besides the fun thing, what else?"

Number 2: *happy*. Okay. Well, of course, I mean look at number one: we're "fun."

Number 3? You ask your kids for three months and they will never say what mine said: *colorful*. Colorful? I think that's a slam.

Number 4: *artsy*. My whole world is crumbling and my bride-to-be is sitting across the table saying, "Oh, so we're colorful and artsy . . . great."

Number 5: *loving and kind*. And at this point I am ready to call it a day. I think I technically win because if God isn't loving and kind, I don't know who is.

Number 6: *readers, learners and storytellers*.

Number 7: *artful*. I said I think that goes under number 4: artsy. They are really reaching now.

Number 8: *forgiving*. "Tania, God is forgiving!" No dice.

Number 9: *funny!* I said, *"We already have fun and happy!"*

Number 10: *nonviolent*. Now, how bottom of the barrel are you when the kids say, "Well, we haven't really killed anybody."

Coming in at number 11: *spiritual*.

Number 12: *religious*. Both of these answers came after a ton of prompting. It was almost like I was a contestant on the $10,000 Pyramid.

"Okay, dear," I said, "we'll go find a religion."

So we went on what we now call "The Beck Family Church Tour." Man, did we see some churches. Did you know there are some churches in this country that don't even mention God? We went from church to church and the kids were loving it—because there's nothing the kids love more than going to church on Sunday.

Things Kids Love More Than Going to Church on Sundays:

Dentist drills

Early bedtimes

Brussels sprouts
Watching Fluffy getting hit by a car

We went to a Unitarian church. We went to a Presbyterian church. We went to a Unity church. We pretty much did everything this side of Satanism.

We enjoyed the synagogue, that was cool. Services are on a Saturday, you get in, you get out, and the rest of the weekend is yours. Of course, you have to listen to a language you don't understand, but hey, I was willing to give it a shot. Tania said no.

Then Pat called. "Are you really doing a church tour?" he asked. "Yes, Pat, we are."

That was when he pulled out the cannon: "Glenn, how long have we been friends?"

"Obviously too long."

"How long have we been friends, Glenn?"

"A long time, Pat." I knew what was coming.

"You owe it to me. You owe it to me to make a stop at the Church of Jesus Christ of Latter Day Saints."

"Sorry, Pat, you just missed us. We've been going in alphabetical order and you should have come in right after B'nai-i-Jacob."

"Remember *The Silence of the Lambs*?"

"Okay, Pat, because of you, I will go. But I want to emphasize that the dogs of Hell could not drag me into Mormonism. You people are nuts and have far too many rules. But I'll go as a favor to you. So what time is it, Pat?"

"Well that's a great attitude to go with. It's Sunday from nine till noon." *Whoah whoah whoah!* Everybody else gets in and out in an hour. You get one hour just like all the others." Because my attitude at this point was, if you can't get the God job done in an hour, your God just ain't strong enough.

So we went with the kids and on the way I said, "Don't let anyone talk to you, because they'll hypnotize you or something! We're in, we're out, we hit the Dunkin' Donuts and I have my feet up on the couch by 10:30. Okay, gang?"

Oh yeah, I was right. They started with that "Mormon Voodoo" right off the bat. As soon as we walked in everyone was . . . *friendly*. One of them, who later became known to my family as "the Amazing Mr. Plastic Man" even told me that he *loved us*.

Please, there are times even I don't like us, how could you possibly *love* us? I was thinking, "Spend some time with me pal and I'll cure you of that."

I thought for sure it was Pat, who was now back in Salt Lake City, on his church telegraph tapping out messages in Mormon code: GLENN AND FAMILY ARE COMING SUNDAY. STOP. BE NICE. STOP. WILL ATTEMPT TO LEAVE AFTER FIRST HOUR. STOP.

He was right.

After an hour, we were heading for the door. I had done my duty. I'd fulfilled my end of the friendship obligation. "Dunkin' Donuts, one light and sweet please—extra large—after all, I just spent an hour with the Mormons."

BE NICE. STOP. WILL ATTEMPT TO LEAVE AFTER FIRST HOUR. STOP.

Oh! Why did these people have to be so nice? And why did Tania have to stop and be nice right back? It cost us our escape window. We were so close to the door, it was right there! I actually could begin to see the warning label: COFFEE IS HOT.

So we sat in on the next class: Gospel Principles. I don't remember what the teacher was talking about, I had no idea really what was going on, but the teacher was talking—*"blah blah blah"*—when all of a sudden, someone raised a hand and said, "Hey, I don't understand that."

I looked at my wife then at the teacher and I looked back at my wife, and I said to her like the Cheshire cat: "Wait a minute. You can ask questions here." I looked at my watch and muttered under my breath, "We'll be in the car in five minutes."

She looked at me, jammed her elbow in my ribs and said, "Don't you dare embarrass me." Still smiling, I raised my hand, and I said, "Excuse me, I've got a question."

I was ready with my question that gets me out of every single church, because this is the question on which every religion to me falls apart. The teacher said, "Yes, Mr. Beck?"

I queried, "Where's Gandhi?"

Silence.

"Pardon me?"

"Where is Gandhi? You know the guy from India? Most religions say something like "Well, you know, Gandhi seems like he had the whole loving each other thing down. He was a good guy—he had a problem with pants, but other than that seems like he was a good guy. The kind of guy who would hang out with Jesus, but he didn't accept Jesus as his savior *so he must be burning in the fires of Hell!*"

I repeated "Where's Gandhi?" And she said, "Well, who

would like to answer that?" Now I am thinking, you're letting *them* answer this question? Maybe I didn't talk down to
you enough. . . . Did I mention I went to Yale briefly?

They explained to me that Latter Day Saints didn't believe
in Hell as others do. There are three degrees of glory as different as the sun is to the moon and the moon is to the stars.

"Gee," I thought, "I have read that somewhere."

A fellow student said "If a dad asked his son to live a good
and decent life and attend Yale Medical School, and the son
did everything that had been asked of him, but he went to
Harvard instead, would a loving father condemn him just for
going to a different school?"

I said, "Well, wait a minute, didn't Jesus say there is no way
to the Father but through him?"

"Yes, that is true," replied the student, "But would it be fair
for one who never had the chance or opportunity to accept
Him to be banished to that lake of fire?"

Follow up your honor, "Are you telling me that Gandhi
hadn't heard of Jesus?"

"No, what I am telling you is that while certainly Gandhi
knew of Jesus, it is doubtful that he ever had the opportunity
to hear the fullness of the Gospel."

This resonated with me because of the many years I had
been stalked by God. Had Pat not been the one to finally turn
the key, would my Father in Heaven have continued to stalk
me or had my chances all been exhausted? Latter Day Saints
do not believe that your chances cease with death. They only
cease with full understanding and denial of truth by your own
exercise of free will. And even then there is no "lake of fire."

I had my keys in my hand, standing up, ready to go. But I listened and said, "Oh, you know what? That kind of works for me." So I sat back down and I listened some more.

Another reason to sit back down and listen some more came as we were leaving; my two daughters said, "Can we go back there?"

What?

"Can we go back there?"

"Um, okay."

My eldest daughter Mary who has always had a gift of the spirit said, "I just feel so warm inside."

So we came back. Pat was very happy. We came back and I kept asking questions.

At one point I had the bishop with his head in his hands, saying, "Glenn, I don't have the answer to that question. I don't think the president of our church has ever been asked that question." But he and others helped me search for the answer only to hear me respond, "Good, I've got six more questions for you just like it."

I took these guys through the ringer. Within a month I had exhausted the resources of Mormon.org and had moved on to *Mormon Doctrine,* a book more akin to scholarly use than light reading. It's like the difference between reading about something in *USA Today* or *The Economist.*

I had firmly believed that religion was only about power and money. And there didn't seem from the outside to be a faith that had a stricter doctrine than the Mormons. I couldn't be part of a religion that was a sham. I wasn't going to join a faith that was about manipulation, superstition, mysteries, greed and money. I like scientific thinking, and I wanted it all to fall into line. For me to join, it needed to logically *work and bear good fruit.*

The Amazing Mr. Plastic Man

The true turning point for me came when we were sitting with the Amazing Mr. Plastic Man. Well, that's what I called him because he was so happy. Nobody could be that happy without being made of some sort of plastic only found deep in the vaults of Hasbro. We were sitting in the elder's quorum, a Sunday school class, discussing Zion, the Mormon concept of a place and condition where "all are pure in heart." It is a place where we can all make as much money as we want, where we can all still be capitalists, but we only take the amount that we need and give the rest to help the poor, widowed or fatherless. Where we really care about each other. Where every single heart isn't forced to do something. Where every single heart *wants* to do something. Wow.

We spent an hour talking about Zion, being pure in heart and all that encompasses, and Mr. Plastic Man got to the end and said, "Now brothers, how do we do it?"

How do we *do* it? How does it *happen?* How is it possible that this could actually happen?

People raised their hands and gave their answers. Then Mr. Plastic Man welled up and said, "There's only one way this will happen: if I truly love you and you truly love me. If deep down inside of ourselves we see people for who they really are, our literal and spiritual brothers and sisters. When we ignore what's on the outside, we don't see what they are doing, we see what's on the inside, and we automatically love them. We may not like them, we may not like what they're doing, but we love them." He was crying and I was crying. Simple truth. Not God in theory but God in practice.

That is when I realized that Mr. Plastic Man was not plastic at all. He was the most genuine person I had ever met; I had just been so corrupted that I couldn't believe he was real.

I had spent months, months mocking this man and calling him the Amazing Mr. Plastic Man, because I couldn't understand him. It was then that I decided, "I don't care if you guys have Kool-Aid to drink in the basement, give me a cup. I'm so tired, I can't live with the baggage of my life any more. I can't live with the mistakes that I have made. I'm laying down my sword, because I want to be like the Amazing Mr. Plastic Man. I want my family to be like his Amazing Plastic Family. I don't care how much work it takes, that's how I want to live and those are the kind of people I want to surround myself with."

"You will know them by their fruits."

Later I called my friend Pat with one more simple question I hoped he had the right answer to: "Will you come to town? Will you baptize me?" He did.

Pat baptized me as a Mormon on October 23, 1999. We must have stayed in those waters for at least ten minutes, because every time he would start to say those words we would just break down. It had taken a lot of time and effort to get to that point and we both recognized the impact this simple ceremony was about to have on me and my family's life.

I stood there in the water testing Him. I told the Lord, "I'm tired, man. I can't do it anymore. I want to be a *nice* person. I want to *like* people. I want to like *me*. But I feel like I can't, because of all this stuff from my past. You've said that if I do these things you will carry the load. Well, I am taking you at your word. If you are God, you are handcuffed to your promises."

That is the great thing about God. He *is* chained to the truth. If He says do *this* and I promise *that* will happen, it must be true or He ceases to be God. I found that out later when I "tried on" tithing.

My life changed while under the water that day. My focus changed. I changed. The guy firing people because of the Sharpie was dead and buried. Where I was only focused on Money, Booze, Business and Cars, I now only wanted to focus on Family and People.

Even now at my radio appearances my "handlers" have to pull me out of the crowds. I love meeting my listeners and would rather be with them than on the stage.

That first year after baptism I spent one day a week trying to find my own little piece of Zion in my house by volunteering at the "bishop's storehouse" (the Mormon version of a church pantry or soup kitchen).

I have also been called to serve in my church in many other ways, including being a home teacher. All men of my faith are asked to do this. We visit families (I currently am assigned three, once a month, to check on them, help them with whatever they require and bring them a Gospel-based message. At first I hated this because I thought it would be a waste of time, wondering what "they" would get out of it. As it is with all service, I now realize that I get more blessings then the recipient could ever receive.

We also are encouraged to participate in what is called "family home evening." We spend one night a week, Monday, playing, learning, sharing and praying together as a family. I have found that it doesn't really make a difference what we do on Mondays, as long as we are all together focused on one another.

It's just putting your family first.

Just a couple of these Gospel principles in practice can change your life and will in turn change your family, friends, community and country. For years I studied and knew the words of Christ as perhaps you do. But it wasn't until I *applied* that faith that my family and I changed.

It always amazes me when I meet people who think I've been hypnotized by those evil Mormons, like somehow a missionary with a bike showed up on my front porch one morning, and by that evening I was baptized. The conversation always begins, "Glenn, I really respect the way you examine every issue and always do your homework, but you just haven't done enough homework on this issue." I always laugh, because out of all of the issues in my life, there is nothing that I more thoroughly examined or prayed harder about than my spiritual journey. Somehow, these people have only received the information on my church from those who are against it. It would be like if I were thinking about buying a Ford, and I only talked to the Chevy dealer. What do I expect the Chevy dealer to say? Believe me, when I bought this car, I

talked to the Ford dealer, then I talked to the Chevy dealer, and I even talked to a Dodge dealer. Then I went back to the Ford dealer again with more questions, because nobody knows a Ford like the Ford dealer. And while it may never be your choice, I did my homework, and after months and now years of study and investigation, I know what I found to be true.

It always seemed like a tough lifestyle to live: "What, no coffee?" But I would gladly give up all of Colombia for what I get in return. It really wasn't as much hard work as I once had thought.

I just came home. Home to a place that helps me and my family live in the Real America.

CHAPTER 11

The Flame That Burns in the Real America

It was a beautiful fall morning on the edge of the land created through divine providence: Coffee shops were open, children were on their buses and people were easing into another typical workday, when suddenly the children and grandchildren of America's greatest generation heard the call. Several times before we ignored that call and drifted back to sleep, muttering, "I know, I know, I'll get up in a minute." But on September 11, 2001, we finally awoke and realized that there is work to do.

The things that we valued on September 10 are not the things we valued on September 12.

After 9/11, we instinctively shed our garish values. We were, for a short period of time, the Real Americans. The fireman's boots were full at every stoplight, yet we still rolled

our windows down to give the firemen more. We stood in line at the blood drives, we said hello to people, we looked them in the eye, we hugged those we didn't know and we actually listened to the answer when we asked, "How are you?"

We didn't have to try to be these people . . . we just *were*. We reached into the bottom drawers of our souls and put on our most comfortable faded jeans.

I too had a change of perception during those days shortly after September 11. I now believe that the greatest generation is always the one that is living in the here and now. It isn't just the generation of our parents and our grandparents. The only question is when are we going to wake up and recognize our greatness?

The spirit of our parents and our grandparents hasn't died out—it's a flame that flickers in all Americans. It is there and is ready to blaze to life as soon as we are ready to face the challenges that lie at our feet.

That flame is what sets us apart, it is what built us, it is why our borders still teem with the poor, the tired and those yearning to breathe free.

That flame burned with zeal in the hearts of millions of immigrants from every corner of the earth who come in search of a better way of life.

The flame that Lady Liberty holds is the American spirit, which burns deep within all of us no matter what our race, our gender or our religious background.

Since September 11, the world has been watching us. That's nothing new, it always has. Since the dawn of man, people have dreamed of a better life, a better way—of freedom—but it was Americans who finally found a way to build it.

Out of that freedom, we have built powerful machines, computers and, yes, weapons of mass destruction—hardware and software that we spend millions on every year to protect and keep secret. But our biggest secret—the one the world wants most of all—isn't a secret at all. It's something we freely give to the rest of the world, and while it seems simple to us, for some reason it can't be duplicated. It can only be passed on from person to person, torch to torch. It is our spirit.

Those of us who weren't trapped in one of the towers that fall morning or on a plane or in the Pentagon have a reason to humbly give thanks. Not for our lives but because we are truly the lucky ones.

God has *not* forsaken us. He's awakened us.

Standing at the bottom of the stairs, he's gently called out, "Kids, it's time to wake up."

We have been given another chance.

Thousands of years ago, in Babel, a great civilization in its arrogance built a tower to reach the sky. It crumbled and the people were scattered. Our hard and steely symbols of power and wealth may have crumbled, but we were not scattered.

Let the world recognize through our actions here and now that those firefighters in New York were not the exception. They are the rule.

Americans don't run from burning buildings. We run *into* them.

The task before us may be daunting, but we are a stronger,

more prepared nation. The torch has been passed, and we are now the greatest American generation. The American spirit is alive and well, and our flame has not burned out. It had just been dimmed a little while we were asleep.

That flame still burns in the Real America.

Epilogue
Stories from the Real America

I had been on the road, traveling across the country to host the Rallies for America. My trip across the heartland brought me to Kansas, where I was going to speak at an air show to welcome home the 190th Air Refueling Wing from the war in Iraq. Although the air show was in the afternoon, I decided to get up early and take a walk around Topeka, Kansas.

It was a beautiful day. The dew was still on the grass that morning, and a crisp, cool wind blew across the plains. Somebody had told me there was a farmer's market near my hotel, so I began to stroll along the wide, quiet streets of Topeka, Kansas.

As I stood on one corner, preparing to cross the street, a woman with a young child in tow approached me. Now, being from Philadelphia, I did what we all do on the East Coast: I said, "Hi, how are you?" expecting her to say, "Fine."

She didn't say, "Fine." She said, "Well, actually, I'm pretty good. We're going to the park today." She continued, telling me her plans for the rest of the day. And my first thought was, "This woman is insane! Run for your life!"

The light turned, and I got about halfway across the street before I realized she wasn't insane—she was just *nice*. That's what the heartland is all about. The clowns in Hollywood and Washington, D.C., can learn a thing or two from Topeka.

After I strolled through the farmer's market, I continued my walk, heading toward the state capitol. A few blocks away from the capitol building there was an old woman walking down the street.

"Good morning. How are you?" I asked her.

The woman stopped. Immediately I thought, "Holy crap! I think she might be crazy too. She wants to *talk* to me."

The old woman said, "Well, I'm doing all right. But I hurt my rotator cuff a little this week. I went to the doctor, and he said I might have to have some surgery. I have an appointment scheduled on Wednesday, though. Wednesday at 10:30. The doctor's gonna look at it again."

She paused, and then she asked me, "What are you doing here in Topeka?"

I told her I was from Philadelphia and I explained to her that I was in town for the air show.

"Philadelphia? That's a beautiful city," she said.

"Really, have you ever been there?"

"Nope, nope. Never have. Though I've heard it was a beautiful city."

As she spoke, she noticed a man walking down the street. I had no idea if they knew each other, but the old lady stopped the passerby and said, "Excuse me. This guy's from Philadelphia. He's coming in for the air show."

So what did he do? The man stopped and said, "Really? You're from Philadelphia? What a fine, fine city that is. That's a beautiful city."

Being a big, fat dummy, I asked, "Have you ever been there before?"

"No sir, I haven't. But I hear it's a beautiful city. Yes it is."

That morning, I wasn't in Topeka, Kansas. I wasn't even in Kansas. I was in the Real America.

What follows are some stories sent to me from citizens of the Real America. If you have one, submit it on my website, www.glennbeck.com.

The Woman in the Restaurant

I am the proud mother of two sons currently serving in the U.S. Army. My youngest son, Matthew, was working as sous chef in a small French restaurant outside Washington D.C. He loved his work and wanted nothing more than to be a chef, but he felt the call to serve his country and so enlisted and left for boot camp in November 2002.

Matt's graduation from Fort Benning, Georgia was scheduled for Feb. 12 and Feb. 13, 2003. His two sisters, his girlfriend and I anxiously piled into the minivan and drove non-stop from Philadelphia, Pa. to Columbus, Ga. The first morning we attended Family Day ceremony, where the graduating trainees wore their Class A uniforms and receive recognition for having "turned green" as soldiers and having learned the army's seven values: Loyalty, Duty, Respect, Selfless Service, Honor, Integrity and Personal Courage. After a brief emotional ceremony the soldiers were released to their families until 9PM that evening.

As the excited young men left the base for the first time in nine weeks, the majority were thinking of food. Most headed for Kentucky Fried Chicken or an all-you-can-eat buffet, but my son wanted to find a nice quiet restaurant, comparable to where he had once worked, and be served a full course meal in style. Two of his fellow soldiers and their families decided to join us. We found a quaint place called the Garlic Clove in downtown Columbus. The staff quickly put tables together for our party of ten, and we enjoyed wonderful service and a wonderful meal and didn't worry about the cost. The three soldiers, still not full after steaks and appetizers and everything in between, decided to splurge on dessert. As the waiter brought various tortes to our table, he informed us that our bill was paid in full; someone wishing to remain anonymous had picked up the tab for our entire party!! We sat there dumbfounded—who would do that? Can you imagine paying for ten full-course meals in a pricey restaurant? We looked around. There were a few scattered patrons in the next room, but basically the place was deserted.

My son asked the waiter if he could please reveal who had been so generous, as he and the other soldiers really felt that they needed to at least say thank you. The waiter pointed out a middle-aged couple in the corner of the next room. The three young men went to speak to them as the rest of us waited in the lobby. When the boys returned they were visibly moved, to the point of fighting back tears. They said the woman began to sob as they approached. She said she started to cry when she entered the restaurant and saw the three of them in uniform, so handsome, young and proud, laughing and sharing a meal with their families. She told her husband right then that she had to do something so the boys would know that someone appreciated them. She was proud of their sacrifice and that they had volunteered to serve their country on the brink of war. She shared that her own husband had been a fighter pilot in Vietnam and when he came home he was spit on, and she didn't want these boys to know that pain.

Matt and his friends were eager to get back to base and tell the story to their drill sergeant. The next morning we reunited for the graduation ceremonies. Throughout the festivities of that afternoon, the conversation kept returning to "that woman in the restaurant." The drill sergeant advised the boys to never forget her kindness and someday when they saw an opportunity they must pass on the kindness.

That evening I said goodbye to my son as he and the others prepared to leave for their next duty station. It had been a whirlwind, emotionally jam-packed two days surrounded by good, loving, honorable, and respectful people. I was thinking of how proud and impressed I was by all our young soldiers and their wonderful families I had met and the inspiring events and ceremonies I had witnessed. As I entered my hotel a copy of

USA Today was lying on the front desk. The headline said that thousands worldwide were protesting against President Bush and the impending war. There were pictures. I stared in disbelief. It was like I had walked into another dimension, some freaky parallel world. That can't be going on! No, that's not how people really feel! It can't be! I've seen the real America. I'm in it. It's all the families bursting with pride watching their sons graduate to the strains of John Philip Sousa. It's that woman sobbing in the restaurant—she's the real America.

> Virginia Weber
> Philadelphia, PA

Ernie

I was born and raised in a small farming town in Northeast Ohio. This was the sort of town where everyone knew everyone else. There were 33 in my high school graduation class. The first day of hunting season, the school would have a teachers' workshop, because most of the boys and some of the girls would not be there anyway. It was a time when you might bring a gun to school in your car, because you were going hunting after school with one of your friends. One of your teachers might come out to the parking lot to have a look at your gun. Got the picture?

Ernie was a farmer like most people who lived in our town. I don't know how old Ernie was. To me he was always old. His wife taught second grade. She was the only one who did and she taught not only us but also some of our parents.

Ernie was never the kind of person you would call friendly.

He never talked much to or about any one as far as I knew. All of us kids had respect for Ernie and would always stop in to ask permission to hunt on his land. With some people you could just leave a note on the porch if they were not at home letting them know you were hunting in their woods. You would never do that with Ernie. He wanted to look you in the eye when you asked, but he always said yes.

Ernie was the sort of man that would walk five miles to collect a dollar that you owed him and he would walk ten to pay you one he owed you. Ernie was old, tough, weathered and respected.

The spring of 1961 was wet, and the crops were going to be late going into the ground. When this happens you can hear tractors running all night, all day and on Sunday too.

There was only one gas station in our town, and that was where the news was spread, at least by the men and boys. The women had some other place that we didn't know about.

The news we heard was that Ernie was working one of his fields and his tractor caught fire. While he was trying to put it out the gas tank exploded. He was in the hospital in bad shape and might not live. We all thought, "That can't happen to Ernie, he's too tough to die."

Someone at the gas station said Ernie would never be able to get his crops in this year. Someone else said "I am going to go to Ernie's on Saturday and plow one of his fields, could one of you boys maybe come up there with a disk?" (A disk is a seed planter that drops the seeds.) I volunteered.

Saturday morning I drove our tractor with its disk to Ernie's farm. The man with the big tractor was already at work pulling three plows. On his second pass there were six furrows and that was enough to start disking (dropping seeds). The field was long with a small rise in the middle. I made my turn at the end and started back. Coming over the rise was another tractor, a different one; he too was pulling three plows. Man I am never going to keep up with two guys plowing I thought. On my second pass there was another tractor with a disk coming over the rise. Ha, I thought, we are going to push those plow guys now.

Then came another tractor with plows and another with disks and harrows, and grain drills. There was a pickup truck at the end of the field with five-gallon gas cans on the back. I heard that the gas station pumps had a glitch that day and none of that gas got rung up.

At lunchtime we all went back to Ernie's house and someone had pulled one of his wagons out of the barn and parked it under one of his big shade trees. Around that wagon was a crowd of farm women, and on it was more food then you can believe.

After lunch we were back to the fields. Remember the glitch with the gas pump? Well, it must have been contagious because the invoice for the seed and fertilizer must have been misplaced and was never seen.

Ernie's wife was at the hospital by her husband's side all that day. When she came home that night there was a little mud in the driveway. I guess she didn't notice. No one locked his or her doors then. I bet the laundry was done too. And every one of Ernie's fields was planted.

Ernie did get out of the hospital in time to start cultivating.

The last time I saw him he was still old, tough and weathered. Sometimes it's hard to tell, but people like Ernie and communities like ours still exist in the Real America.

Nick Brockett

Marietta, GA

Christmas in Georgia

The year was 1981 in Augusta, Georgia. I was a single mother of 2 very young children living in a small trailer and no vehicle. All my immediate family was living in Texas and I was very much alone. This was before all the benefits that are now available to others finding themselves in the situation I was in.

I had a job as a bookkeeper with a reputable tire company. There were just 3 white people working there, myself, the owner and a manager. Prejudice against blacks was very much alive. All labor was done by the "boys," and they never earned a penny over minimum wage. If there was no business to be done, such as changing a tire or fixing flats, then the "boys" were told to dig a hole. After it was dug then they had to fill it back up. In the beginning, my only contact with them was when they were ordered to park my company car or carry my briefcase. I was told to not talk to them.

I was appalled at the way humans were being treated so needless to say I rarely followed my bosses instructions. I could never treat another human as a "slave" or a possession. After awhile the "boys" learned to respect me and even protect me from some of the trouble and men that a business like that bought in. After awhile I even told the men that if they went

out of their way to be nice to the boss, he might start to come around a bit and treat them with respect.

Christmas was coming up. The men pooled their money together for a present for our boss. They collected enough to get him a leather jacket.

Ten days before Christmas my boss propositioned me. Five days later (five days before Christmas) I was fired for turning him down.

I was looking forward to my paycheck to buy Christmas presents for my children. But my boss refused to give me my final check. I was completely distraught, and had no idea what to do. I did not want to call my parents because they had sent me $100 weeks before for my birthday, and I had bought a hobby horse and bike with training wheels for the kids. Five days before Christmas and all I had was 2 presents and not even a tree to put them under. I asked God to help me.

Christmas Eve, just as the sun was setting, I received a knock on my door. The "Boys" of the Tire Co. were standing at my door with their hands full of presents, food and a tree. I didn't even know they knew where I lived! I was shocked, happy and crying.

What made this even more special for me is that most of these men did not even make enough money to support their own families. When I asked where they could get the money for such a wonderful surprise I was told they took the leather jacket back for a refund and then added some more money of their own.

Being American is not your ethnic background. It is attitude, love, compassion, and so many more things that are good and right. It is being human with integrity and morals. I will never forget what the men did for me and my children. Every Christmas I say a special prayer for them and always try to help someone else in need to pay back the blessings that god bestowed on me.

What happened to the tire company? The business eventually closed down. I never found out what happened to the owner, but I pray for him, too.

Sharon Carpenter Buhrts
La Vernia, TX

Acknowledgments

I find myself at a dichotomy. There have been so many people in my past who have helped me get where I am. I really should write an acknowledgments page and list the people who have helped me get here. One that jumps right off the top of my head is the person who raised me for most of my life and has been married to my father for over twenty years, my amazing mom, Dee.

But if I start on this list, then I'll inevitably leave out people like Kraig Kitchin, Gabe Hobbs, Sean Compton, Michael O'Shea and Charlie Brown. So the people like Greg Novack, Peter Tripi, Rich Bonn and John Clark will be pissed that I mentioned the people like Louise Burke, Trevor Oliver, Dan from NOC, Fiona, Nicole, Myshala and Bill Rogers from

PETP. People like John Hogan and Jack Swanson will be like, "Hey, if you mention Phil Boyce, Sue Treccase and your sister Coletta, you better be mentioning Lowry Mays, Mark Mays and Jeff Fisher." I can just picture people like Dave Dalley, Dan Andros, Neira Jackson and Glen Campbell walking around angry at me just because I forgot to mention Phil Azoon, Linda Hiltzik and Randy Michaels.

Can you even fathom what would happen if I forgot to mention my editor, Mitchell Ivers? I mean, this guy was stuck on an RV with me for a full week while we drove cross-country and wrote a book at the same time. Not only that, but we completed the whole thing in record time! That's not an editor, that's a magician. I'd really look stupid if I forgot him.

That's why I'm not going to mention Lisa Paige (Burguiere), Miramax Matthew, the Brandon 2nd Ward, Nick Michaels, or even my daughters Mary and Hannah. It wouldn't be fair to Jack Welch or my dog Veektor. And I don't want to have to reveal too much by thanking Britney Spears, for that night. She must move on. She's young, her heart will heal.

If I started naming people like my brother Jeff, or Amir Forester, or Troy from *Star Trek* or Cathy Hawks, then I would have to name everybody, like Grace Blazer, Mark Commune, Wilifred, Dan Mandis, Michael Altmont, Jim Dingle, Dr. Atkins and his evil nemesis Ronald McDonald, plus Brian Glicklich, Domino Theodore, "Mike," Robin Bertolucci, Jack, Ted and Sharon.

But even if people like Bishop Robert Howell or my sister Michelle, Jake, Gabe, Jacquelyn and Beau weren't upset about not being included in the acknowledgments section, I would feel badly about leaving out John and Amy, Flemlaski, Velveeta, Jack Daniel's, Johnnie Walker, Jennifer Barrett, Jennifer Eccleston and J. Lo.

And then there's Jeremy and Makell Boyd, Mike Hagans, the entire Premiere Radio Networks staff, WFLA News and the entire continent of South America, who should be mentioned as well as the state of Ohio, Felix the Cat and that guy from the bus this morning.

Just imagine if I ran into the entire Southington Ward on the street. They would probably yell something like "Hey Glenn! Why didn't you mention Amy and Adam? Or what about Claire McCabe, the mother of your children?"

I could only reply by saying that I can't believe I forgot to thank Vinny and MaryAnn Colonna or Gwyneth Paltrow or everyone who helped with Stuff-A-Bus and the Rally for America.

If I did do an acknowledgments page, I could just list names of important people I don't even know, like Rush Limbaugh, Lee R. Raymond, Henry Kissinger, Ronald Reagan, Alan Greenspan and also Ben *and* Jerry just to make me sound important.

I could say that I'd like to thank ClearChannel Communications for providing me with such close ties to the Bush Administration. We all share in the benefits of that personal relationship, but my friends Sam Adams, Bud Weiser and the Insiders really love it.

And I'd have to mention the one person who I would be nothing without: Wayne Newton . . . oh yeah, and the

woman I'm going to travel through the eternities with, my wife, Tania.

Of course, I wouldn't be able to name some people (you know who you are), but that is just because it would be an inside joke between us. Ha ha ha. You know what I'm saying, _____? (Insert name here.)

Honestly, why bother with acknowledgments of other people, when the truth is that there is only one person responsible for my success: me. Only me, all me, me me me. Thanks, me! Thank you for being . . . you . . . me.

Author's Note

To hear more about Glenn Beck's Real America, listen every day on a talk-radio station near you.

Or, listen online worldwide at www.glennbeck.com.

Get a one-month free subscription to the GlennBeck.com Insider, which includes:

- Streaming audio of the show with behind-the-scenes bonus content
- News of the day
- Thirty-day show archive with no commercials
- Favorite audio clips on your own schedule, including classic bits
- Glenn Beck webcam
- Message boards

To sign up for your free month, go to www.glennbeck.com/therealamerica.